Introduction

Witches come in many forms and variations with differing views on and approaches to the practice of Witchcraft. Some call themselves Wiccans, others witches, still others use the term Pagan. One thing most of us have in common, however, is the belief that magic is real. Not the kind of magic in which a stage magician pulls a rabbit out of a hat, either, but the kind that anyone can use, with or without a magic wand or special words like *abracadabra*. (Not that either of those things will hurt ...)

What is magic, then? We can't see it, but we can definitely see the results when it works. We can't touch it, but it most certainly can touch us and those around us. For lack of a better definition, let's say that magic is a form of energy that science has not yet found a way to measure, but which many of us believe is as real as gravity and electricity.

Belief is at the heart of a witch's practice.

Whether you believe this energy comes from the gods or from the universe or from some other source altogether, for the sake of this book, we'll agree it is out there, and we can tap into it to make positive changes in our lives and in the world around us.

And this, my friends, is where spellcraft comes in. Spellcraft is the art and craft of using the energy of magic. Like any other art or craft, it can take time and practice to get good at doing it, and some people have more of a natural gift for it than others. But anyone can do it. You can do it, I promise.

Like everything else in Witchcraft, there are numerous different approaches to casting spells. They can be very simple or extremely elaborate and complicated. Take minutes or days or even months (if you are repeating the same spell over a long duration in order to get a specific outcome). They may call on specific deities, the universe in general, or simply be sent out into the world with good intentions and lots of hope. And what works for one situation may not work for another, so it is likely you will end up exploring a number of options and styles over the years as you walk your magical path.

That's where this book comes in. Within these pages, I will talk about some of the basics of spellcrafting, the things I have discovered over the years that work for me, and those that don't. Your mileage may vary, of course, and what is right for me won't necessarily be right for you, but hopefully you will find at least some of the contents helpful as you follow your own spellcrafting journey. At the very least, you should have some interesting times experimenting and trying to find out what suits your own magical style.

There are tips and activities to get you started, or to keep you growing and learning if you've already been on this path for a while. Plus, with any luck, you'll have some fun. Using magic, while a serious business, can also be entertaining and fulfilling and empowering. Tapping into that mysterious energy only works if you also tap into your own internal magic—intent and desire, focus and determination, hope and belief. All these are aspects of spellcrafting too.

Don't be discouraged if you don't feel as though you have mastered spellcrafting, especially if you are fairly new to Witchcraft. There is a section that will help you discover how to write your own spells, if you don't already, and plenty of spells I've written for you to use either as is or with your own variations.

Remember that practice will help strengthen both your abilities and your comfort with casting spells. It will also help you discover which types of spellcasting you like, and which ones seem to work best with your own particular beliefs, skills, and limitations.

With or without the magic wand.

Chapter One
SPELLCRAFTING BASICS

In the introduction, I said that spells are a way of tapping into the power of magic. How you do this will depend on a variety of circumstances: how much time you have, how much privacy you have, the amount of energy you can spare on that given moment on that given day, which tools you happen to own, and so on. It may also depend on your own personal style. Do you like things simple or do you enjoy pageantry and lots of beautiful extras?

But let's start with the basics first. A spell is a set of words, usually spoken aloud, although they can also be written. It can be as short as a single sentence, or a couple of pages long. Usually it falls somewhere in the middle. A spell can be a prayer or a meditation, but it is usually asking for something.

To a witch, there is no such thing as coincidence, and everything happens for a reason, even if we can't always know what that reason is.

That something might be as simple as peace of mind or protection for the ones you love as they travel, or as complicated as a request for the perfect job that needs to fit a specific set of requirements. What you're asking for and how much help you need will also affect the type of spell you use and how you approach casting it, as will your level of experience (folks who have been practicing magic for a long time may not need as many tools or as detailed a ritual to help them focus).

Intent, Will, Focus, and Belief

Whether you've been casting spells for two days or twenty years, there are four main components to spellcasting that everyone needs. They may seem simple, but without them, your spell is unlikely to work.

INTENT——Before you set out to cast a spell, you need to have a clear idea of your intention (what you want to achieve) and how you plan to go about achieving it.

WILL——Will is the strength you put into a spell, as well as your commitment to follow up with concrete practical actions afterward.

FOCUS——Focus is how you channel your will into your intent during the spell. If you find focus challenging, using tools may help. Most people also find it becomes easier to focus over time, with practice.

BELIEF——The belief that magic is real and that your spell will work. This is at once the simplest element and sometimes the most difficult to achieve. But if you don't believe, your spellcasting is unlikely to succeed.

Creating Sacred Space

Sacred space is where a spell is cast, usually a temporary circle created for the duration of the ritual, although

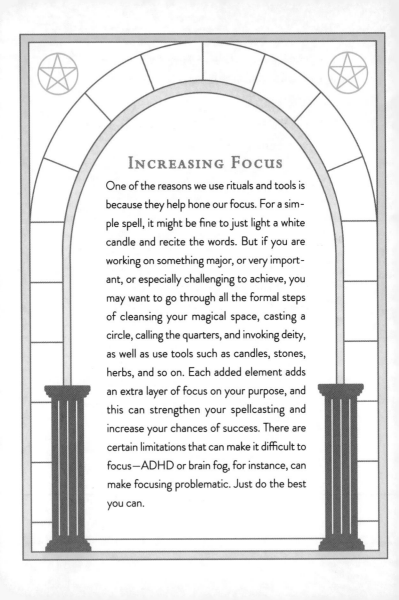

Increasing Focus

One of the reasons we use rituals and tools is because they help hone our focus. For a simple spell, it might be fine to just light a white candle and recite the words. But if you are working on something major, or very important, or especially challenging to achieve, you may want to go through all the formal steps of cleansing your magical space, casting a circle, calling the quarters, and invoking deity, as well as use tools such as candles, stones, herbs, and so on. Each added element adds an extra layer of focus on your purpose, and this can strengthen your spellcasting and increase your chances of success. There are certain limitations that can make it difficult to focus—ADHD or brain fog, for instance, can make focusing problematic. Just do the best you can.

some people have permanent sacred spaces set up either inside or outside of their homes that are used for magical work on a regular basis.

For instance, I have a traditional nine-foot circle of stones set out behind my barn where my group, Blue Moon Circle, has been doing ritual for over twenty years. But we still often go through the formal steps of creating sacred space for each individual ritual, because the act of making sacred space helps put us in the right frame of mind for spellcasting, and reminds us that we are in a "bubble" of magical energy, outside of the mundane world.

There are a number of steps to creating sacred space, and not everyone does every step or uses the same exact approach each time they prepare to cast a spell. There are variations that work better for individual spellwork, and some that are more useful for spellcasting with a group. It also depends on your personal preferences and the spell you are going to do. Creating sacred space can be as simple or as elaborate as you desire, but will probably include one or more of these elements.

CLEANSING——One of the ways to prepare a space, whether it is in the middle of your living room or in your backyard, is to cleanse it physically or energetically or both. You definitely don't want to cast a spell in the midst of clutter, so if necessary, you might want to tidy and sweep. You can also use a magical broom (one kept specifically for ritual work) to sweep the circle clear of negative energy. This can also be done by burning cleansing herbs or incense, spritzing with a mixture of salt and water, or even ringing a bell.

CASTING THE CIRCLE——This is when you formally delineate the area in which you will be doing the magical work. You can achieve this by walking the perimeter of the space, or putting down something that will physically represent it (a length of yarn laid out in a circle, for instance, or sprinkling salt around the edges), or simply by visualizing white light all around you. If practicing with others, someone may actually walk around the outside of the circle with a broom or a staff or an athame. Or you might cast the circle "hand to hand," where the first person takes the hand of the person to their left, and then that person takes the hand of the person to their left, and so on until everyone has joined hands and the circle is complete. Creating a circle, movement is always deosil, or clockwise (in the Northern Hemisphere).

Some people like to say something aloud, such as, "I am in sacred space, between the worlds, safe and protected as I do my magical work." Others simply get on with their spellwork.

> The full moon is considered the most powerful time of the month and is always an appropriate time for spellcasting.

RELEASING SACRED SPACE——

When you are done with your spellcasting, you will want to open the circle and return to your regular life. Most often, this is done by reversing whatever you did to form sacred space in the first place. If you swept the circle, for instance, you would sweep in the opposite direction (widdershins, or counterclockwise) in order to open it. If you visualized a wall of white light going up, then you can visualize it coming down.

··· ACTIVITY 1 ···
Practice Creating Sacred Space

One of the simplest ways to manifest sacred space is through visualization. Try practicing this as often as you can, and you will likely find it becomes easier and easier over time, until it is practically second nature. Find a relatively dark and quiet room where you have an open space at least big enough to turn around in. Close your eyes for a moment and take a few deep breaths, grounding and centering yourself as much as possible. You can have your eyes open or closed for the next part, whichever works best for you.

Put your right arm out with a finger pointing away from you and visualize a white light coming from the tip of that finger. Turning slowly clockwise, draw a circle at around chest height with your finger, visualizing the light drawing a circle as you turn. When you have come all the way around, see in your mind's eye the light joining together and spreading both down and up, enclosing you in a bubble of softly shining light. Feel the difference in the space where you are standing, safe and comforting, and the space outside the light. Visualize that glow for a few minutes, and then turn clockwise and see it dropping or fading away.

The Four Quarters and Beyond

One of the components of ritual usually performed after creating sacred space is "calling the quarters" or "calling the directions." They are sometimes referred to as the watchtowers in traditional forms of Wicca. There are four quarters: north, east, south, and west. The quarters are each associated with a different element, and we call in those elemental powers to protect our circle and boost the energy of our magical working.

Each element is also associated with different colors, attributes, and so on, although not every Witchcraft tradition will necessarily agree on what those are. Here are the basics:

NORTH——Earth. Green or brown. Grounding, growth, abundance, prosperity, nature, physical and financial issues. Winter and midnight.

EAST——Air. Yellow. The mind, thought, intellect, knowledge, psychic work, purification, and clarity. Spring and dawn.

SOUTH——Fire. Red. Passion, energy, creativity, courage, healing. Summer and noon.

WEST——Water. Blue. Flow, flexibility, emotions, love, fertility, the subconscious. Fall and twilight.

Some people start by calling the east, while others start with the north. Either way, you move clockwise (deosil) around the circle and call each one in turn. It is also possible to call them all at once, although that isn't how it is usually done. Quarter calls can vary from the very simple (*I call the power of the East to watch over my circle and lend me its strength and protection*) to the more elaborate (*I call the East, the power of Air, to blow away old patterns that no longer work for me and to leave my mind clear and focused*).

I like to use quarter calls on the sabbats that are specific to that time of year, such as "I call in the soft spring breezes to blow away the stagnant energy of winter" at the spring equinox, but you can do them any way you choose.

Some people also call in additional directions, using the sky above and the land below. The sky is associated with clarity, wisdom, and energy, and the land is associated with grounding and energy from the earth.

Invoking Deity

After you have called the quarters, the next step in ritual is usually to invoke deity. This can take different forms depending on your practice, which gods and/or goddesses you follow (if any), whether it is a full moon or a sabbat, and whether or not the spell you are casting is directed at one particular deity.

This might sound complicated, but really it isn't. You just need to figure out which deity or deities will work best for the spell or ritual you are doing, and which ones you feel a connection with. Some people simply say "God and Goddess" and don't specify any one by name. That's just fine. That's what I do much of the time. But sometimes you will want to be more specific. Here are some suggestions for deciding how you are going to invoke deity, but it always comes down to what works best for you.

> Unless you have already found one on your own, it can be helpful to research the various gods and goddesses often associated with a Witchcraft practice to see which ones appeal to you the most.

GODDESS ONLY—On the full moon, we generally only invoke the Goddess, because it is her night. If you want to call on a goddess by name, try one of the lunar goddesses, like Selene or Diana.

GOD AND GODDESS——For sabbat rituals, we usually invoke both God and Goddess and often call on those who are specifically associated with that holiday, such as Brigid at Imbolc, or Hecate at Samhain. Usually when we invoke both, we use deities from the same pantheon (Greek, for instance, or Celtic), but that isn't a rule. Eclectic witches, who draw from many different cultures, may mix and match, as it were.

SPECIFIC DEITIES——If you are doing a spell that aims at a particular goal, you may wish to invoke a deity or deities who are associated with that attribute. For instance, if you are doing a love spell, you might call on Venus, whereas if you are doing a spell for prosperity and abundance, you could invoke Ceres, who is a harvest goddess.

PERSONAL DEITIES——Some witches have a deity with whom they feel a personal connection. A patron or matron god/dess is someone you worship on a regular basis. So, if you follow Diana, for instance, you may call on her no matter what type of spell you are casting.

Invoking Deity

Keep in mind that, unlike the quarters, which we summon, the gods are not in any way our servants. Always invoke them with respect and politely ask them to join you in your magical work. And remember to thank them when your spellwork is done.

Your invocation could be as simple as, "Great Goddess, Great God, please join me in my circle and lend your power and wisdom to my magical work," or it can be more complicated and directed at a particular deity. But no matter which approach you use, all you can do is ask nicely and hope they will listen. In my experience, they usually do.

The Dos and Don'ts of Spellcasting

There are a few things to keep in mind as you send your spell out into the universe.

- *Be careful what you ask for.* Spells are powerful. When they work, they can bring amazing results. Make sure what you wish for is really what you want. Because later, it may be a lot more difficult to undo the spell than it was to cast it in the first place.

- *Harm none.* Not all witches follow this rule, or believe it is necessary, but I do. In part because I believe in the Law of Returns, but also because I just don't like to put out anything negative. I'd rather do protection magic than hexing. This is a personal choice, but one you will want to consider carefully before casting a spell.

- *The Law of Returns.* While there are some witches who don't believe in this, many do, including me. This rule says that whatever you put out into the universe comes back to you. (Some people even believe it comes back times three.) So you want to be careful what you send out, lest you get something back you really don't want.

- *Respect the free will of others.* One of the core tenets of modern Witchcraft is the belief that all people have free will. This means we are responsible for our own actions. The universe may throw challenges at us, but how we deal with those challenges is up to us. But that also means we have to respect other people's right to make their own choices, even when we don't agree with them. In magical work, this means you should never do a spell that will affect another person without their permission. This includes love spells, which should never be cast on someone else, and even things like healing spells. Always ask first, and if the person involved says, "No, thank you," that's their right.

- *Be very cautious when doing weather magic.* It can be tempting to do a spell for rain if your garden, or your whole county, is suffering from a drought. But weather magic is tricky. If you call in rain, you may be depriving someplace else that needs it even more. Or ruining someone's wedding day. Or you may get a storm that is more destructive than helpful. This is one area where I tend to leave things in the hands of the gods. The only exception is that I will do protection magic if a bad storm is coming.

- *Be even more cautious when doing love spells.* Think about it. Would you want to fall in love with someone because they cast a spell on you? I don't think so. And if you cast a spell on someone to make them love you, how will you ever know if their love is real, or only because you made them feel that way? Remember the rule about free will. You can cast a spell to be open to love, or even to ask the gods to send love your way, but never cast a love spell on a specific person. Seriously, ask me how I know. Take my word for it that it is a bad idea. (Yes, I too was a newbie witch once.)

- *Keep your requests reasonable.* There's a reason you don't read about a witch winning the lottery every week. And it probably isn't because there aren't a bunch of folks out there casting that particular spell. The gods help those who help themselves, and they are much more likely to answer a request for something reasonable, like a better job or boost in general prosperity.

- *Make sure you're not casting a spell when there are everyday solutions available.* Spells are a wonderful tool, but you don't always need to use them. For instance, if you are looking for a new job, there are practical approaches you can take. If these don't work, by all means cast a spell, but you might not need to start there. And even if you do end up using spellwork, make sure you follow it up with more mundane efforts. Spellcraft is powerful, and you want to make sure you save it for the times you really need it.

Deity Lists

Unless you have one specific god or goddess you call on all the time, it can be handy to have a list of which gods are associated with particular kinds of spellwork. This way, when you need to cast a spell, especially if it is something last minute, you don't have to go searching for the information. Do a little research (there are plenty of Witchcraft books that talk about this, including some of mine) and have a list prepared for the next time you want to do some spellwork for prosperity, healing, safe travel, or whatever it is you have in mind. As a bonus, you'll probably learn some interesting things about deities you're not already familiar with, and you might even find one that resonates with your own particular practice. (Hint: there is a very basic set of correspondences at the end of this book that includes deities. That's a good place to start.)

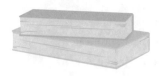

Chapter Two
CASTING A SPELL

Now that we've discussed some of the core basics of spellcasting, it is time to talk about preparing to cast an actual spell. Some of these elements will vary from spell to spell depending on the complexity of any particular spell, the magical style of the person casting it, or even what you're in the mood to do, but here are some important points to consider before you create sacred space or light the first candle.

What Is Your Goal?

This is without a doubt the most important part of spell-casting. If you don't have a goal firmly in mind, your spell is doomed to fail. Unlike tarot reading, where it is fine to ask something vague like "What do I need to know today?" when you are casting a spell, you need a concrete goal.

That can be a bit tricky at times because you want to be precise about what you are asking for while still leaving the gods and the universe enough wiggle room to fulfill your wishes in ways you may not have thought of or anticipated.

There will be some cases where what you are casting a spell for is fairly specific, such as a successful surgery, or safe travel, and that's fine. At other times, however, you may want to lean in the direction of being more open in your spellcasting. For instance, say you need to have more money quickly to deal with an unexpected expense like repairing a car. You *could* do a spell for the money itself, and that might work.

Or you could cast a spell for prosperity in a more general way

No matter what some may say, it is fine to do spellwork to benefit yourself as long as it doesn't harm anyone else.

and ask the gods to help you find a way to get the car repaired. This might open up a number of options, like someone volunteering to fix the car for you, or an unexpected gift, or something else being paid for, thus freeing up money to spend on the car.

Of course, if you are writing a spell yourself, you will have more options for how general or specific you are going to be with it. If you are using a spell written by someone else, garnered from a book or online, you will just have to pick the spell that best suits your goal.

You may want to write your goal down to make sure you are focused on it and have it clear in your head before casting the spell. Some people find this helpful, while others don't need it at all.

What Tools Will You Use?

The answer to this question can be "none" or "all of them" or anything in between. Remember that magical tools help create focus and power during the casting of a spell, so some of your answer will depend on how complicated the spell is, your current state of mind (it can be harder to concentrate when you are upset), how experienced you are at spellcasting, and, of course, if you are someone to whom focus comes easily or not.

For some people, maintaining focus during a spell isn't an issue. For others, it can be a real challenge. If you are one of the latter, you may wish to use more tools than someone for whom it isn't a problem, especially if you are fairly new to spellcasting.

Of course, tools are also just plain fun. Who doesn't like pretty crystals, bright-colored candles, and a fragrant assortment of herbs? For many witches, using various magical tools makes them feel powerful and more in tune with their Craft, so they can serve multiple purposes.

Nonetheless, it isn't always necessary to use tools when casting a spell. There are circumstances when you may not have them handy, like when you're traveling or away from home or when the spell is simple enough that they don't seem necessary. There are plenty of times during the full moon when it may be sufficient to stand outside in the moonlight or feel the moon's energy from wherever you are inside. Some people also prefer a simple approach, in which case they may not want or need tools.

For me, if a spell is uncomplicated and easy, I may just light a candle and stand at my altar. I tend to save the tools for spells where I need to pull out all the stops, or the times when I'm practicing with my coven. When I first started out, I used a lot more tools, so it is also a matter of experience. And personal choice.

Here are some of the more commonly used tools witches utilize in their magical work:

CANDLES——It is always appropriate to use a plain white candle. As with many things in Witchcraft, certain candle colors are associated with specific goals, so you may wish to use a green candle for prosperity work, or a blue one for healing. Candles can also be etched with your goal or intentions, anointed with magical oils, and so on. But don't panic if you don't have the "right" color candle. White is always fine, and if you feel like the spell calls for a purple candle, go for it. It is always more important to listen to your own instincts than to follow what I or anyone else writes in the spell instructions.

HERBS——Witches have been using herbs for magical purposes since the dawn of time, as far as we can tell. Some of them have actual practical uses, such as healing, but they also have associations with goals, so there are some that are said to be the most effective for love spells and others for protection. Many have multiple uses, so it is good to have a variety of the basics on hand, if you can.

STONES AND CRYSTALS——Like herbs, different gemstones have various magical qualities associated with them. If you like using them, you will probably want to have at least one for each type of spell you are likely to be casting, maybe more. Also like herbs, many stones have multiple correspondences, so you don't necessarily have to have hundreds of them, unless you want to. (Warning, many witches find crystals addicting and end up with lots of them all over the house. Mind you, I'm not saying this is a bad thing.)

CLEANSING HERBS AND INCENSE——There are various tools you can use for cleansing your space, yourself, or your other tools, but many people like to use incense, sage, or other cleansing herbs like sweetgrass or lavender. If you use these at the start of your spellwork, they can help you get in the proper frame of mind for magical work, especially if you use them most of the time you do spellcasting. Sage, a popular choice, has become problematic due to overharvesting and

WORKING
WITH STONES

Crystals don't have to be large and
expensive in order to work. Smaller tumbled
stones are just fine, and if you want something a
little fancier, you can usually find reasonably priced ver-
sions of the more valuable stones like amethyst in crystal
points or clusters. Most stones have more than one attribute, so you can start out with a few basics that are good
for a lot of things and expand your collection over time.
If you can only have one stone, start out with a nice
quartz crystal. They're reasonably inexpensive and
a good power booster. Even a decently sized
one shouldn't break the bank.

issues with cultural appropriation. If you choose
to use it, I encourage you to seek out ethically
harvested products from
Native retailers. Be
careful when using
incense or herb bundles
inside. The smoke can be
overpowering at times,
and some people have
sensitivities to the
artificial scents found in
many incenses.

> If you have a favorite
> color, check on its
> magical associations to
> see if there is a reason
> you are drawn to it.

DIVINATION TOOLS—Witches sometimes do
some form of divination during their spells,
either as an aid to the spell itself (like focusing
on a particular tarot card that represents your
goal or laying out runes for the same purpose) or
as part of the magical working itself if they are
looking for answers. Common divination tools
include tarot cards, oracle cards, rune stones,
scrying mirrors, and pendulums, among others.

ATHAMES, WANDS, AND STAFFS—These three
tools are generally used to point or direct energy,
or both. For instance, when calling the quarters,

you might use an athame or a wand to point in each direction. They can be used to direct energy when casting the circle or to draw magical symbols in the air or on the ground. Which one—if any—you use will depend on which style appeals to you most. Some witches have all three, some don't use any of them and simply point with a finger instead. Athames, wands, and staffs are very personal tools and can be as simple or as decorative as you choose.

CHALICE OR CUP—A fancy goblet or a simple cup can be used to hold the "ale" part of cakes and ale (this can be anything from water to wine to juice to actual ale) to be sipped from at the end of a ritual or poured out on the ground as a libation in honor of deity.

CAULDRON—Cauldrons can be small and portable or large and stationary. Often made from cast iron, mini cauldrons can be useful for burning small items (like a piece of paper) or holding candles or offerings. Medium or large cauldrons can be used to mix magical ingredients or burn more sizeable items. Cauldrons can also be made from copper or pottery.

MUSIC AND MUSICAL INSTRUMENTS—You may not think of music as a tool, but spiritual practitioners have been using it for centuries in every culture there is. Whether it is drumming, ringing a bell, playing a flute, shaking rattles, or even chanting, music can induce a trance state, or lift the spirits, or help raise energy within a magical circle. It has even been used for healing. If you are practicing with others, drumming together in circle can be amazingly powerful, but if you are on your own and don't feel like trying to create music yourself, there are plenty of witchy drumming and chanting CDs and downloads available.

BOOK OF SHADOWS AND JOURNALS—Many witches like to keep track of their magical work. Some use a Book of Shadows, also known as a grimoire, and others simply use a journal or a notebook. When I started out in my first coven, my high priestess gave us lots of handouts, so I actually decorated a three-ring binder with dried flowers and witchy symbols and used that.

BROOM OR BESOM—Brooms have long been associated with witches. A besom is simply an older style of broom, usually made from twigs. They are used for moving energy and cleansing a magical space, not for actual cleaning.

· · · ACTIVITY 3 · · ·
Pick Your Tools

If you are just starting out with a Witchcraft practice or if you have been walking the path for a while but want to expand your spellcasting abilities, it can be a good idea to figure out which tools you are the most comfortable with and which ones seem to work best for you. Or if you are perfectly happy casting spells without using tools at all.

This is mostly a matter of experimentation. Try doing some spells without any tools. Then try a few various combinations like one crystal and one herb, or multiple crystals and herbs and a colored candle, and see which ones help you focus best. Which tools make you feel the most powerful? Which ones just feel awkward or unnecessary?

Only you can figure out which tools will best suit your own personal approach to spellcasting, and it is worth paying attention as you practice and keeping track so you can use that information in future magical work.

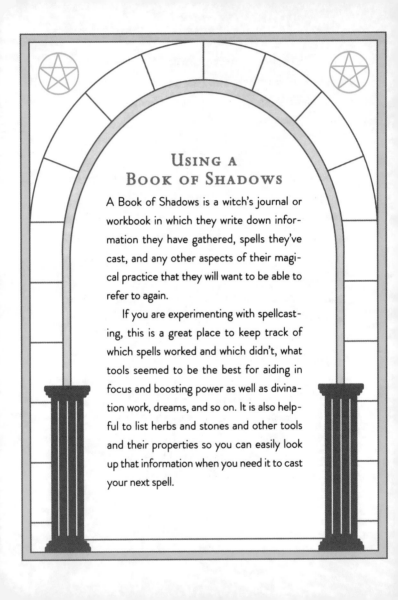

USING A BOOK OF SHADOWS

A Book of Shadows is a witch's journal or workbook in which they write down information they have gathered, spells they've cast, and any other aspects of their magical practice that they will want to be able to refer to again.

If you are experimenting with spellcasting, this is a great place to keep track of which spells worked and which didn't, what tools seemed to be the best for aiding in focus and boosting power as well as divination work, dreams, and so on. It is also helpful to list herbs and stones and other tools and their properties so you can easily look up that information when you need it to cast your next spell.

How Complicated Do You Want to Get?

This is definitely something you want to consider before you pick a spell to use or write your own. If you are writing your own spell, you can always create something that is as simple or as complicated as you want, but if you are using a spell written by someone else, you will want to pick one that suits your taste and the circumstances under which you will be casting it.

After all, if you only have five minutes to spare, you don't want a spell that takes ten minutes of prep time, dozens of esoteric and hard-to-source ingredients, and half an hour to perform. On the other hand, if you enjoy the deeper, more complex spells and feel they boost your magical abilities, you probably won't want something that says, "Just light a candle and say the spell." If there is a spell you like that is too simple for your tastes, you can always add your own extras.

You don't have to pick one style or type of spellwork and stick to it every single time, but you may want to consider the following on a case-by-case basis and use the answers you come up with to help you decide how complicated a spell you want to do in that particular instance.

- How much time do you have to do the spell?

- Do you have a variety of supplies on hand or do you need to use a few everyday items?

- Are you going to have enough privacy to work a long, complicated spell?

- Do you prefer things that are simple and easy to do? Or do you enjoy magical work that requires more elaborate ritual?

- Do you have a few favorite spells (either your own or those written by others) that are useful for what you need, or do you have to start from scratch?

- Is your request (whatever you're doing the spell for) urgent and/or important?

There is no right or wrong answer here. Just what works for you. But it can be helpful to answer this question before you get started.

Picking a Day and Time

Sometimes the day and time are irrelevant. If you need to do spellwork *right now*, the day and time will have to be what they are. Your intention and will are the most important things.

DAYS OF THE WEEK FOR SPELLCASTING

Monday—The Moon. Healing, sleep, peace, friendship, purification, psychic work, goddess worship.

Tuesday—Mars. Protection, passion, courage, victory, energy.

Wednesday—Mercury. Communication, intellect/the mind, study, wisdom, knowledge, answers, travel, change.

Thursday—Jupiter. Prosperity, money, business, goals, success, abundance, work issues.

Friday—Venus. Love, friendship, beauty, arts and crafts, nature, blossoming.

Saturday—Saturn. Endings, mysteries, homes, boundaries, banishing.

Sunday—The Sun. Power, success, strength, god worship, protection.

On the other hand, if you can be flexible and the spell-work can wait until the optimal moment, you may wish to pick a specific day and time to cast your spell to get the best possible energy behind it.

For instance, many witches like to practice spellcasting based on the phase of the moon. The waning moon (from the day after the full moon until the new moon as the moon grows smaller in the sky) is generally used for decrease or spellwork to get rid of or lessen things. The waxing moon (from the new moon until the day before the full moon as the moon grows larger) is used for increase or spellwork to bring in or have more of things. So if you were doing spellwork for prosperity, you might use the waning moon to get rid of debt and the waxing moon to ask for a better job, a raise, or some other way of bringing in more money.

Some Witchcraft traditions also associate different types of spellwork with particular days of the week, so that is something to consider when you are deciding when to cast a spell. Additionally, some people like to do

> The most important thing about writing a spell is your focus and your intent, not getting the words perfect.

spells for new beginnings at dawn and endings at dusk. As always, there are no rules, just what feels right to you. But these are good starting points if you are just setting out on your spellcasting journey.

· · · ACTIVITY 4 · · ·
Matching Your Spellwork with a Day or Lunar Phase

You can do this one of two ways. Either pick a day or a lunar phase and find an appropriate spell to perform during that time, or pick a goal you wish to do spellwork for and choose the best time or day to perform that spell. If you keep a Book of Shadows, you might want to make a note of what you did and how you felt it worked. If not, just pay attention and see if you think the timing made any difference.

Alone or With Others

There are two types of Witchcraft practice: solitary and group. (Okay, there are a zillion types of Witchcraft practice, but we're looking at this particular topic now. You've got to start somewhere.) Solitaries generally do spellwork on their own, and group witches often belong to a coven or magical circle. But even those who belong to a coven often do some magical work on their own, and some solitaries occasionally take part in a group ritual if they have access to one.

Some of this depends on what's available to you or what your personal inclinations are. For instance, although I am a fairly solitary person by nature, it turns out that I very much enjoy being part of a magical group, and I have been practicing Witchcraft with others since my introduction to the Craft many years ago. However, I still do plenty of spells on my own as part of my own personal practice.

Your situation may mean you don't have the option to do spellcrafting with others, or you may just prefer not to. But if you have the choice, it is worth considering whether any given spell is something you'd rather cast on your own (it may be deeply personal or not something others would connect to) or with others (general spells like prosperity, healing, protection, and the like will usually appeal to a number of people, even if their goals or intentions aren't exactly the same as yours).

One advantage to casting a spell with others is that when the circumstances are right, you can generate an amazing amount of power. Of course, if you cast a spell on your own, you don't need to focus on anyone other than yourself.

What Happens Afterward

There are a couple of aspects of post-spellcasting that are worth looking at other than the obvious hoping that your spell accomplished what you set out to do.

The first is one of the general tenets of Witchcraft that is often taught as part of Wicca, but which I think applies no matter which Witchcraft path you happen to follow. It is said that when you cast a spell, it involves these four elements: To Will, To Know, To Do, and To Keep Silent. We've already addressed the first three earlier in the book, but the fourth one is also an important concept.

It doesn't mean you can't mention the spell you've cast to anyone under any circumstances. If you practice with others or have witchy friends, you can certainly mention that you've cast a spell to achieve your goal. But it can be tempting, especially if you are new to Witchcraft, to tell everyone you know what you're doing or brag about the powerful spell you've just cast. Resist the inclination to do this, if you can. Not just for the obvious reason that it simply isn't cool or might get you into trouble, but also because the act of talking about your spellcasting can actually weaken the magical work you've done. Think about it this way: you directed all your energy into your spell. Every time you mention it, you steal a little bit of that energy away, sending it out in another direction. This completely defeats the purpose of casting the spell in the first place.

The other "after spell" aspect to consider is how you follow up the magical work with action in the mundane world. It isn't enough to cast a spell for prosperity, blow out the candle when you're done, and sit around waiting for the gods to hand you a winning lottery ticket. (I wish.) The gods help those who help themselves, and they expect you to work toward your goals after the spellcasting is over.

> Magical protection is a wonderful thing, but don't forget to take as many practical measures as you can to keep yourself and those you love safe.

So if you are doing a spell for prosperity, you may want to go out and look for a better job, or think of ways to advance yourself at the one you have, or find side gigs that will bring in money or ways to make the money you have work harder for you. If you did a spell for healing, consider what practical steps you can take to work on your health while you are waiting for the spell to work: eat better, exercise more, focus on mental health, eat more chocolate . . . oh, maybe that one is just me. But you see my point.

It isn't enough to just cast a spell. You have to give the universe the best opportunities to grant your desires, and that means following up by putting your own energy and dedication into whatever your goal is.

Chapter Three

HOW TO CREATE
YOUR OWN SPELLS

There are many wonderful books out there filled with spells just waiting for you to use them. I know, because I've written a few of these myself. (And have a bunch by other people on my shelves.) Plus, there are a bunch of spells included in this book too. There is absolutely nothing wrong with using a prewritten spell, as long as you can find one that suits your needs, and not everyone is comfortable writing their own.

That being said, there are a few reasons why you might want to try your hand at creating your own spells, at least on some occasions. I promise you, it is easier than you think, and there are a number of ways in which it can benefit your magical practice.

Why Write Your Own?

There are lots of reasons to use prewritten spells—they're faster, easier, and you don't have to stress over whether or not you got them right. But Witchcraft isn't always about what is fast and easy, and sometimes it pays to put in a little extra thought and effort. Here are a few examples of why and when you might want to consider creating your own spell.

- *Spellcrafting is part of being a witch.* Not that it is required; you're still a witch if you never write your own spell. But it is an element of magical work and one you might wish to try eventually, even if you're not comfortable doing it when you start out.

- *Sometimes your goal is very specific.* Many of the spells you find in books are fairly general so they can be used by the most people possible. This makes sense. But if you need a spell that isn't covered by your average spell book, you may need to create your own that will be perfect for your needs.

- *Writing your own spell can be very powerful.* The more of our own energy we put into any spellwork we do, the more powerful it will be. In a perfect world, we would all grow our own herbs, make candles from scratch, and so on. Obviously, that's not possible for most people (although almost anyone can have a few pots of commonly used magical herbs on a windowsill). But when you create your own spell, searching for the perfect words and honing them to best meet your goal, you are putting lots of extra energy into that spell, and that can only be a good thing.

> There is nothing more personal than a spell you have written yourself.

- *It can be fun.* Seriously, once you get past being intimidated by the process (if you even are—some people are naturals and dive right in), it can be fun and rewarding to create a spell from scratch and use it in your own magical practice. If it is really good, you might even consider sharing it with others.

• • • ACTIVITY 5 • • •

Write a Spell

Don't worry too much about getting it perfect. Just enjoy the process. Start by figuring out your goal for the spell. Prosperity, healing, and protection are always good places to start. So let's say for example that you want to do a spell to protect your home. Figure out which tools you want to use, if any. (A piece of red jasper, for example, and a black candle inscribed with protection runes.)

Sit down and write the spell. It doesn't have to be long. My spells range anywhere from four lines to forty. Just do what you're comfortable with. Read the rest of this chapter to help you decide whether or not you want it to rhyme, which deities (if any) you want to call on, and whether it is something you want to do once or multiple times. Then just play around with the words until it feels right to you.

To Rhyme or not to Rhyme, and Other Questions

You have a number of options when you sit down to write a spell, and before you start searching for the right words, you will probably want to make a few decisions first. As with most other aspects of practicing Witchcraft, there is no wrong way, simply whatever feels most comfortable or "right" to you.

- *To rhyme or not to rhyme?* A lot of people worry about being able to make their spells rhyme. It isn't really that difficult if you keep your ending words fairly simple, and often I only rhyme every other line, which makes it easier yet. But there are some spells that seem to flow more smoothly if you don't have rhyming, so it will really depend on the words and the meaning behind them. It is traditional for spells to rhyme, because the beat and rhythm is said to make spells more powerful. Personally, I think the way the spell feels when you say it is more important than whether or not it rhymes. Try it both ways and see. You'll see plenty of examples of both in this book.

- *Do you intend to cast the spell at a certain time or on a specific day?* For instance, when I write a spell to be used on the night of the full moon, I might include a phrase in the spell that says so. (Great Goddess, I call to you on this, your night of the full moon, and ask that you grant me these wishes three.) If so, you might want to add that aspect into your spell. Or not, if you will be using it in the future on different occasions.

- *Who will you call on?* Many spells invoke the Goddess and God in a general way (God and Goddess, hear my plea) or call on a particular deity if there is one that is appropriate for the spell. You might want to call on Brigid for creativity or Apollo for healing. If you follow a particular pantheon (Greek, for instance, or Celtic), you might stick to gods from that culture. Or if you have a patron god/dess you worship, you might always call on them. Other people simply say, "Powers of the Universe," or nothing at all.

- *How crucial is the spell?* If your need is great and the spell is very important, you might want to spend some extra time crafting it to make sure your words, and any accompanying actions, are as perfect as possible.

- *Have you got your goal set firmly in your mind?* Your goal, the thing you are going to focus your spell around, should be as clear in your head as you can make it. For instance, if you are looking for a new job, are you willing to take any job you are offered, or are you looking for something specific, like a job that will allow you to be creative or be home in time for your kids to get out of school? Each of these things would require different wording for a spell, so

> Spells don't have to be long and complicated; sometimes the simplest spells are the most powerful.

make sure you know exactly what it is you want. At the same time, remember to leave some wiggle room for options you might not have thought of. Choose your words carefully.

Written or Memorized?

Are you going to be reading the spell or saying it from memory? In general, I don't think it makes any difference to the power of a spell if you read it off a piece of paper or out of your Book of Shadows rather than memorizing it. But if you want to have a spell you can use anywhere without having to carry it around with you, it is usually safer to make it short and easy to remember, unless you are lucky enough to have an amazing memory.

Finding Your Comfort Zone

The most important part of spellcrafting is figuring out what works for you. Just because you know other witches who always write their spells in iambic pentameter and spend hours crafting them to be absolutely perfect doesn't mean that is how you have to approach creating your own spells. If you are a "fly by the seat of your pants" type of person, you will probably want to be more flexible.

To Hex or
Not to Hex

This is a subject on which not all witches agree, and most people feel pretty strongly one way or the other. Hexing is when you cast a spell on someone with negative intent. In other words, the spell is intended to cause harm. There are those who feel that in some cases this is justified because of the actions of the person the spell is aimed at (an abuser, for example).

I certainly understand the temptation, especially in cases of abuse. That being said, I don't do it. For one thing, there's that pesky Law of Returns issue, which doesn't say, "Unless you're right and they're wrong." It just says that you get back what you put out, no matter where it is aimed. Plus, I truly believe in "harm none." Each witch has to make this choice for themselves.

On the other hand, if you are someone who likes to have everything "just right," you will undoubtedly want to apply that approach to your spellwork too.

All the spells in this book can be done either with a full ritual (casting the circle, calling the quarters, and so on) or with nothing at all. Or anything in the middle. If you are just starting out, you may find it helpful to do most or all of the steps of formal ritual to help you get into the right mindset for magical work. Those who have more experience may not find this necessary, especially for the simplest spells if they are done on your own and without others taking part too. It is completely up to the individual and what works best for them.

If you're new to the Craft or spellcrafting, it is a good idea to experiment. Try different ways of creating spells and see which one works best for you. You may discover you like a lot of approaches depending on the situation and the spell you need to cast. Keep an open mind and don't forget to have fun!

chapter three

Chapter Four

SPELLCRAFTING TOOLS

I wrote earlier about the tools we use to help us boost our focus and energy during spellcasting. In this section, I'm going to go into more detail so you are better able to decide which things you want to use and when, and also which tools perhaps don't resonate with you.

Keep in mind that you don't have to use any tools other than your heart, mind, and spirit. You certainly don't have to use them all. Although there's nothing stopping you, if that's the way you roll. Some witches have limited space or funds, and so they focus on the tools that work best for them. Others enjoy trying their hand at a little bit of everything and have cabinets full of candles, stones, and herbs. Okay, yes, that's me. But I've been doing this a really long time …

Anyway, my point is that different witches are drawn to different tools or combinations of tools, and you may want to experiment to see which things work best for your own personal style of magical work. This will likely change over time too. When I started out, I used an athame quite often because that was what the high priestess who taught me used. Eventually, after spending a number of years with my own group, which leans toward the more casual, I stopped using it for rituals, although it still sits on my altar.

Of course, there are many more useful items than I have room for in this book, so you may want to do some exploring on your own to see what else calls to you. In the meanwhile, here are some suggestions for you to try out for your own spellcasting needs.

Candles

Candles are among the simplest and easiest-to-use magical tools. They are readily available and don't have to look obviously witchy if you aren't yet out of the broom closet. After all, most people have a candle or two hanging around, right?

They are also extremely flexible. You can use a giant pillar or a tiny tea light, or votives, or tapers, or candles that have been molded into a specific shape. Because wax is soft, you can etch symbols into the sides to add to their power. They can be anointed with magical oils or rolled in herbs, combining their usefulness with other tools.

Of course, they are also a potent representation of light in the midst of darkness, as well as being a safe substitute for a bonfire when there is no place to have one. Additionally, they are available in many different colors, so you can integrate color magic into your spellwork without having to add in another element.

Remember to be cautious when using candles. Make sure they are in firesafe containers, never leave them burning when you leave the room, and keep them away from pets.

• • • ACTIVITY 6 • • •
Color Magic

There are some general color associations that can be used with various tools, including candles, stones, charm bags, and more. For instance, if you are doing spellwork for prosperity, you might want to use a green candle, a green stone such as aventurine or jade, and your spell written with green ink.

Here is a list of the more commonly accepted color correspondences, although as with everything else witchy, people may have their own variations. (Note that there is some overlap.)

GREEN (AND SOMETIMES BROWN)—Earth, prosperity, success, growth, fertility, luck, grounding, healing.

BLUE—Water, healing, calm, sleep, purification, hope, tranquility.

RED—Fire, energy, courage, passion, sexuality, power.

YELLOW—Air, the sun, intellect, the mind, communication, clarity, creativity, joy, the God.

PINK—Romantic love, friendship, calm, peace, happiness, compassion.

PURPLE—Spirituality, psychic powers, meditation, purification, success.

WHITE—The moon, purification, protection, truth, cleansing, the Goddess.

BLACK——Protection, grounding, power, divination, banishing, binding.

SILVER——The moon, the Goddess, intuition, psychic ability, spiritual truth.

GOLD——The sun, the God, vitality, strength, power, wealth.

Create a spell or adapt one written by someone else and integrate color magic into your spellcasting in whichever way you choose.

Herbs and Plants

Magical practitioners have been associated with herbs and other growing things since the dawn of time. After all, most early witches lived in rural areas where they could readily find the plants they needed growing wild in the forests and fields or tuck them into a back corner of their gardens. It may not be that easy for today's modern witch, especially the city dwellers, but almost everyone can grow a few herbs on a sunny windowsill, and of course you can usually buy whatever you need either fresh or dried.

When we talk about herbs in a magical sense, we don't just mean the plants that are technically classified as herbs, but also trees, shrubs, flowers, fruits, vegetables, and so on. Because they are living, growing entities, plants each have their own particular vibration and energy. When we use them for magical work, we are essentially tapping into that energy and channeling it into our spellcraft.

Individual herbs are associated with different properties, such as prosperity, protection, love, healing, and so on. Often an herb is used for more than one type of magic, so it is fairly easy to pick out a few favorites that will cover the basics and add to your collection over time. One of the things I love about herbs is that they have multiple uses, so the dill you cook with can also be used for love and prosperity, and calendula can be made into a healing salve or added to a magical sachet for the same purpose.

> Some essential oils can be quite expensive, but you can always substitute something cheaper or buy a tiny bottle and only use a few drops at a time.

Remember, just because something is an herb, that doesn't mean it is harmless. Some herbs are dangerous to people or pets if ingested or there is an allergic reaction, so make sure you educate yourself on the properties of the herbs you'll be using.

Here is a short list of some of the more commonly used herbs and the correspondences most often associated with them. Keep in mind that different traditions sometimes have different views on specific herbs, and as always, listen to your own inner wisdom when you are spellcrafting to see what feels right to you.

BASIL—Love, prosperity, protection.

CHAMOMILE—Love, peace, sleep, healing, prosperity, protection.

CINNAMON—Prosperity, success, love, passion, healing, protection, energy, psychic ability, spirituality.

DILL—Love, protection, prosperity.

GARLIC—Protection, healing.

GINGER—Energy, power, prosperity, success, passionate love.

LAVENDER—Purification, love, sleep, calm, healing, happiness.

LEMON—Purification, cleansing, love, energy.

PARSLEY—Protection, purification.

PEPPERMINT—Healing, love, prosperity, purification, psychic powers.

ROSEMARY—Healing, protection, love, concentration and memory, purification.

Sage——Protection, purification, wisdom.

Thyme——Purification, healing, psychic abilities, love, sleep.

• • • Activity 7 • • •
The Magical Cup of Tea

One of the easiest ways to use herbs is by making a tea or an infusion. All this means is you place your chosen herb or herbs into hot water. If you are making tea, you will drink the end result. An infusion (which might be made from plants that are not safe to ingest or that you don't like the taste of) can be integrated into your magical work in other ways, like adding it to a bath, dipping other elements of the spell into it, and so on.

Try picking out a magical goal and then choosing some herbs to make a tea out of that combine well with your intent. For this exercise, pick a few herbs you wouldn't mind drinking a few sips of after you say the following spell. For instance, for healing, you might use chamomile, cinnamon, and peppermint. You can even get the cinnamon in stick form and use it as a kind of wand to stir your mixture. If none of the herbs listed here appeal to you, there are lots more options. Or you can skip the spell and simply visualize your goal as you drink.

··· Spell 1 ···

Tea with Intent

Once you have made your magical tea or any favorite herbal tea you happen to have around, recite this simple spell and take a few slow, mindful sips. You might want to visualize the herbs in the water becoming part of your body and boosting the power of your intent as you send it out into the universe.

> Herbs and water, water and herbs
>
> Joined together in power and intent
>
> Joined together in heat and fusion
>
> To bring about my wish for [your goal]
>
> As I drink, let their power be mine
>
> And let my goal be achieved
>
> So mote it be

Incense and Oils

In a way, incense and oils are a subset of herbs since they are usually made from some kind of plant. Of course, many incenses are created with artificial chemical scents, but I don't recommend those for magical use, since the entire point is to tap into the energy of the plants, and if you don't use something natural, there is no energy to tap into. (It's fine to burn that kind of incense if you just like the smell, but it doesn't add as much to your spellwork.)

I like to use incense made from essential oils, which contain the concentrated plant, such as lavender, rosemary, or any number of other lovely scents that also have magical associations.

Incense is used during spellcasting to represent the element of air, and occasionally both air and fire, since you light it. It can also be used as part of the spell itself as a way of sending your intentions out into the universe, carried by the smoke. It comes in the form of sticks, cones, and even coils, and you can buy all kinds of fancy incense holders to use with it if you want to.

Magical oils can be made up of one essential oil or a combination of a number of different ones. The correspondences are the same as the herbs they are derived from, so the previous list (as well as those in other Witchcraft books) will help you pick which ones will be most helpful for any given spell. If you are buying premade oils, they may or may not have the combinations of plants you prefer, but it is super easy to make your own. Once you bless and consecrate the oils for magical work, you're good to go. Again, make sure you are using essential oils and not fragrance oils, which are chemical and artificial and have no magical properties. I make my own magical oils using essential oils added to a neutral base, such as jojoba or olive oil, but you can find premade magical oils for sale at Pagan stores or online.

Oils can be used to anoint candles to boost their power, added to charm bags, used to anoint yourself before beginning magical work, dropped on a crystal or amulet … their uses are nearly endless. I especially like to use them for healing and protection spellcrafting, but you can try using them as part of any type of spellwork.

If using oils to anoint candles, be sure to avoid getting them on the wick, because they can be quite flammable, and always make sure to put the candle in a firesafe container in case of flare-ups.

• • • ACTIVITY 8 • • •
Create Your Own Magical Oil

This is a fun and rewarding way to add your own personal touch to your Witchcraft practice. Pick two or three essential oils you like the smell of and that smell good together, making sure they are appropriate for whatever magical purpose you are creating them for. For instance, if you want to make an oil for healing, you could mix a few drops each of geranium, lavender, and rosemary. Any base oil will do (almond, jojoba, safflower, grapeseed, even olive oil from your kitchen), although some of them turn rancid faster than others.

Place your carrier oil in a small jar or bottle made of dark-colored glass, then add the essential oils. I like to use a dropper for each essential oil so I can control the exact amount I add. Your magical oil can be closed using a cap or a dropper cap (the bottles can usually be found at health food stores and Pagan stores and, of course, online). Then swirl the contents clockwise nine times, or however long feels right to you. If you want, you can then bless and consecrate the oil for magical use.

• • • Spell 2 • • •
Consecration and Blessing of Magical Tools

This is a very simple spell to consecrate any of your magical tools. You can accompany it with actions, such as sprinkling the tool with salt and water, wafting it with purifying herbs, and waving it over a candle flame, or you can simply recite the spell. For an extra oomph, do it outside under the full moon.

Bless and consecrate this tool

For my magical use

Imbue it with the energies of Earth, Air, Fire, and Water

The blessings of deity and nature

Let it empower and aid me in my work

In any and all positive ways

From this day forth

Crystals and Stones

Crystals and stones are among my favorite tools. I am a self-confessed "crystal junkie," unable to make it out of a New Age store or walk away from a vendor's room at a convention without adding just one more to my collection. But in my defense, they are both beautiful and useful, and there are so many different ones, each with its own particular energy. Also, I'm a Taurus, an earth sign. I'm blaming it on that.

Like herbs, gemstones have specific associations and correspondences with various magical goals. And like herbs, not everyone agrees on what those are, so it is important to follow your own instincts and use the stones that feel right to you for any given situation.

In Witchcraft, we tend to refer to "crystals" in a general way, rather than alluding to the stone's structure, which may or may not be crystalline. Crystals and stones may also include things like amber (actually a resin), jet (a form of ancient petrified wood), and pearls. For the most part, however, when we talk about crystals, we mean various kinds of semiprecious stones that can range from the common agate to the somewhat more distinguished amethyst.

> When picking out a gemstone, hold your hand over each option to see if you are pulled toward one in particular.

But you don't have to take out a second mortgage on your house to use stones in your magical work. While it is nice to have a few larger pieces, smaller tumbled stones will work just fine for spellcrafting if that is all you can afford or have space for. And like candles, crystals can be left out in plain sight without anyone realizing they are part of a Witchcraft practice.

Stones can be used as part of your spellcasting to increase the focus and power of your spell, but you can also channel the energy of a spell into a stone so you can carry it around or put it on your altar afterward. I like to add stones to charm bags, but I also always have a few on my altar and around the room, just because I like their own natural energy.

Container Spells and Witch Bottles

Container spells are an old tradition in many cultures and can serve various purposes. Usually the containers used are glass or pottery with a tight-fitting lid or cork, but technically any magical work where a number of items are placed inside something might be considered a container spell. (I tend to think of sachets and charm bags as their own type of magic, although they work in much the same way. They're more likely to be used for a shorter amount of time, so they don't need to be as sturdy.)

Container spells were often used to capture and break hexes, especially in cultures where Witchcraft was considered to be a bad thing. The original witch bottles, for instance, were designed to keep people safe from witches, although these days they are more often used as a general protection spell *by* witches. For instance, when I moved into my house, I created one and buried it under a brick in front of the entry door so that nothing malignant could pass.

Container spells are usually meant to work over a long period of time (my witch bottle is now over twenty years old!), so you want to make sure the container you use is reasonably sturdy. Some people even seal their container with wax after they've added all the contents and closed it up. Protective spells can be put into wearable amulets, or actual jars can be buried or placed discreetly around the home.

Other examples of traditional container spells include the "honey jar," designed to sweeten someone's attitude, and the "money jar," which is intended to draw prosperity. Items that are put inside containers can include herbs, stones, items specific to the type of spell being cast, or even pieces of the spellcaster's own body such as hair or nail clippings (these are called "taglocks" and are usually used for spells meant to draw something toward a particular person). For instance, a honey jar might contain something sweet, and a protective spell usually has some sharp object meant to impale danger and prevent it from entering.

Once the spell has served its purpose, be sure to dispose of the container and its contents in a respectful way. The container can be washed and reused, and anything inside it can be burned or buried if you have safe ways to do so.

• • • ACTIVITY 9 • • •

Witch's Bottle for Protection

To create this, you will need a small clean jar with a lid or a cork and some or all of the following ingredients: piece of tumbled red jasper or black onyx, dried rosemary, a clove of garlic, two straight pins (or something else sharp and pointy like a sewing needle or a piece of broken glass). If you want, you can also make a miniature scroll from a piece of paper and draw protective runes on it or even write out the spell on it, then roll it up and tie it with string.

Once you have cleansed both the container and all the items going into it, place each thing in slowly and mindfully, focusing on your goal of long-lasting protection for your home and those within it. Place the top on tightly. For an extra touch, you can melt wax around the edges and/or top and draw protective runes into the wax once it is mostly dry.

Recite the protection spell and either bury the jar right outside your home if that's an option or place it near the entrance or on an altar. If you need to hide it in plain sight, consider placing it inside another larger container that simply looks decorative or placing it inside a cabinet.

··· SPELL 3 ···
Simple Protection Spell

This can be used for a protection sachet or charm bag. If you're using something more delicate like fabric, you may want to renew the material and spell occasionally.

Protected by the spirits mighty
Blessed by God and Goddess bright
With this strong and sacred spellcraft
Guard my home both day and night

Brooms and Besoms

You might not think of a broom as a tool for anything other than housecleaning, but for witches, they are not only powerful aids to magical cleansing, they are in many ways a symbol of Witchcraft itself. For this reason alone, some witches have a broom they reserve for ritual work or decorative brooms used to represent their spiritual path.

Besoms are an older style of broom, once used for actual sweeping, although it is hard to imagine a bundle of twigs tied to a stick being very effective. Modern brooms are made from broomcorn (or plastic, but not only are those not very witchy, they don't even clean well), a form of grain. The broom is the only magical tool that combines the feminine (the bristles) and the masculine (the handle), which gives it a special power.

When you are using a broom or besom for spellwork, it is almost always to cleanse your sacred space before you begin performing your magic. (In which case you would always use a broom that is set aside for this purpose.) But miniature brooms and besoms are fun ways to add a magical touch to your home without anyone knowing, and you can also imbue them with magic, like the tradition of placing a broom over the doorway for protection. Brooms are also sometimes used in handfastings, Pagan wedding ceremonies, since it was a tradition for a couple to "jump the broom" to signify they were starting a new life together.

Wands, Staffs, and Athames

If you are wondering what all these tools have in common, besides being generally cool, it is that they are all used during spellwork to point or direct energy. For instance, if you are calling the quarters, you might use a wand or an athame to indicate the directions. You can also use them to draw symbols in the air, like a pentacle, or to guide the energy as you close or open a circle.

A witch's wand, athame, or staff is very much an extension of their own magic and can be an extremely personal tool. Over time, these items are imbued with their user's energy, so they should always be treated carefully and with respect. Never pick up another witch's wand or athame without asking first.

All these tools can be either bought or crafted, and even a store-bought tool can be personalized to make it more your own. Wands and staffs, in particular, can be made from found wood that is more or less the right size and shape. Wands are usually around the length of your forearm, and while staffs can be any size, it is typical to use one that is about the height of your shoulder. Whether bought or found, wands and staffs (and often athames, depending on what the handle is made from) can be decorated in a way that puts your own magical touch on them, including carving, woodburnings, adding crystals or feathers, or anything else that has meaning to you.

Do you need to have one of these? No, of course you don't.

Any tool made with heart and spirit and positive intent will boost your magical work simply because of the energy you put into it.

But they can be a wonderful symbol of your witchy path, and especially if you are just starting out, they can help remind you to focus your energy and direct it in a meaningful way.

Sachets, Charm Bags, and Poppets

Fabric magic can take many forms, but these are three of the most common ones, and they have been used for centuries by witches, herbalists, and healers. With little more than a piece of cloth, a needle and thread, and a few additional items like herbs and stuffing, anyone can create a powerful tool for positive magical work.

Sachets are small pillows, usually made by doubling over a piece of fabric and then sewing two sides together, placing your magical ingredients inside, and then sewing the final side closed. Charm bags are much the same, except you use a ribbon or tie to close it off, creating a small pouch instead of a pillow.

Poppets are slightly different in that they are intended to represent a person (usually the one making the poppet, although they can be done for others if you ask their permission first). The fabric is cut out in a vaguely human form with a head, two arms, and two legs and sewn

EASY
CHARM BAGS

If sewing isn't your thing but you still want to make a charm bag, you can buy a premade taffeta or velveteen drawstring bag or even a simple muslin one (usually found in kitchen supplies), which has the benefit of having a blank surface you can draw on.

There is an advantage to sewing by hand, because you can put your energy and intent into every stitch, but if you need something fast and easy, a premade bag will work just fine. On the plus side, they come in many different colors, so you can buy a mixed set and have them on hand for a variety of magical goals.

mostly shut before being stuffed and closed up the rest of the way.

For any of these tools, you decide on your goal (a dream sachet, for instance, to tuck under your pillow, or a prosperity charm bag, or a healing poppet) and choose the appropriate corresponding ingredients to tuck inside your project. For a sachet, you might also want some form of stuffing, such as cotton balls, tissues, fabric, or pillow batting. You'd definitely use one of those for a poppet, since you need to fill out the arms, legs, and head.

Ingredients can include herbs, small crystals or tumbled stones, symbols of your goal, a piece of paper on which you've written your goal or rune symbols that represent it, or anything else that seems appropriate to you. If you are making a poppet for yourself, you can also include a lock of hair or something else personal.

· · · ACTIVITY 10 · · ·
A Healing Poppet

For this project, you will need a rectangular piece of cloth (you should use a light color if you are going to draw on it), scissors, needle and thread, healing herbs (try calendula, lavender, lemon balm, peppermint, rosemary, or thyme—dried is best if you are planning to keep it around for a while, although fresh herbs can have a lovely smell), a small piece of amethyst, quartz, bloodstone, lapis, sodalite, or any other healing crystal, some kind of stuffing, and a piece of paper and a pen. Optional are yarn for hair and a marker or markers for drawing.

Fold over the cloth at the head and cut out a human figure with arms and legs. If you want, you can draw the figure on the cloth first. Sew the figure about two thirds shut, being mindful of your goal with every stitch. You will probably want to stuff the head, arms, and legs at this point. Place your ingredients inside the poppet and write your name and any symbols you want on the paper, tucking that inside with the rest, then sew it shut the rest of the way. If you want, you can add yarn for hair or draw features onto the poppet's face. You may also want to either sew or draw on the poppet where the healing is needed to direct the energy there. For instance, if you have migraines, you could tie a string around the poppet's head. If there are heart issues, you could draw or sew a little heart in the middle of the poppet's chest.

Then say any appropriate healing spell over the poppet and put it on your altar or someplace safe.

Divination Aids

Divination has been part of Witch-craft since the beginning, although not everyone does it or wants to. There are some forms of divination that don't require anything extra, like reading palms or tea leaves (neither of which I have ever been any good at, incidentally). The rest of the time most people use some sort of divination tool to help them get answers to questions or a peek into a possible future.

> Divination can be challenging, but it can also be fun and useful. The trick is to find the tools you are the most comfortable with and practice, practice, practice.

Cards are one of the most common of these and come in many different forms. Tarot decks are usually a set of seventy-eight cards, often based on the classic Rider-Waite-Smith deck, although these days there is an incredible range of different styles. Tarot cards are fun to work with, but there can be a steep learning curve, so some people prefer oracle cards, which are a bit simpler and still beautiful. Either one can be used for guidance or inspiration or as an adjunct to magical work.

Some witches prefer rune stones, which are an old form of divination made up of twenty-four or twenty-five small tiles or stones usually stored in a special bag or box. These can be made out of anything, from actual stones to clay, bone, wood, or even glass. Some sets are stunningly beautiful and others are extremely plain (I have both and how they look makes no difference to how they work), but they are all blank or merely decorative on one side with a rune symbol on the other side. There are twenty-four symbols, each standing for something different, and they may be etched or painted onto the stones. A twenty-fifth stone, when one is used, is a blank known as the Wyrd, which means the unknown or no answer. Runes are usually pulled out of their bag or spread out on a table upside down and are best used for simple questions.

Scrying is another type of divination, one that involves looking into a black mirror or a dark bowl filled with water and looking for images there. Alternatively, you can use an actual crystal ball if you can afford one that is large enough. Easy yes-or-no questions can be answered with a pendulum, which is basically a string or chain with something dangling on the end, like a crystal, which will move back and forth as you hold it.

Working with Familiars

Familiars are not, strictly speaking, a tool. But like tools, they can help boost your magical energy if you are fortunate enough to have one. Most pets are simply that, wonderful companions who share our homes and our lives. But every once in a while, a witch will have an animal (often a cat, but familiars can take many forms) that shows an interest when magic is performed or a sensitivity to spellwork and ritual.

You can't train an animal to be a familiar—they either are or they aren't. And they rarely take an active role in magical work, but their very presence can add to the power of your spellwork. Keep in mind that you should never force an animal to do anything magical if they don't seem to have any interest in doing so. I promise, the gods wouldn't approve.

Chapter Five
LUNAR SPELLS

Witches do spells at any and all times, depending on their needs. But the full moon is probably the most popular day for spellcasting because magical energies are at their peak. Any spell done on the night of the full moon will likely get an extra boost.

Spells done on the full moon or other lunar dates usually call on the Goddess (as opposed to the Goddess and God) because the moon symbolizes feminine power, and the moon is considered a manifestation of the Goddess

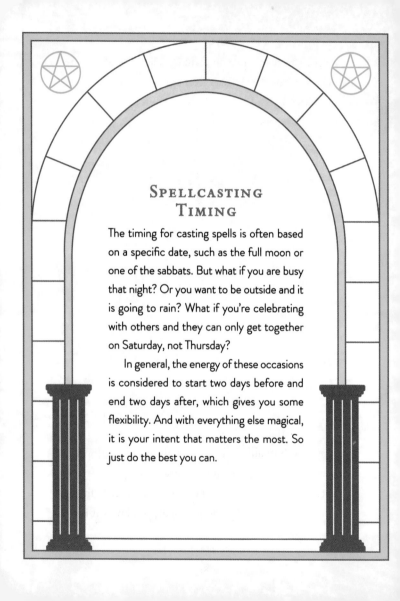

SPELLCASTING TIMING

The timing for casting spells is often based on a specific date, such as the full moon or one of the sabbats. But what if you are busy that night? Or you want to be outside and it is going to rain? What if you're celebrating with others and they can only get together on Saturday, not Thursday?

In general, the energy of these occasions is considered to start two days before and end two days after, which gives you some flexibility. And with everything else magical, it is your intent that matters the most. So just do the best you can.

herself. There are specific goddesses associated with the moon in particular: Diana, Selene, Luna, and Artemis are among the better-known ones, although Hecate is sometimes worshipped on the dark or new moon.

There are a few types of spellcasting that are better left to other nights, like banishing, which might be more effective on the night of the dark moon, but in general any spellwork can be done on the full moon. It is also a good time to simply commune with the Goddess, no rituals required.

Full Moon

If you want to do some form of spellcasting but don't want anything too complicated, try the simple spell below to invoke the Goddess and ask for her blessing.

• • • Spell 4 • • •
Full Moon Shining

All you need is a white candle in a firesafe container, preferably something you can hold in your hands without it getting too hot, although you can always put it down on something if you are going to be inside.

Stand where you can see the moon if possible (although if you are inside or it is a cloudy night, you know it is still there). Light the candle and either hold it up to the sky or place it on an altar or table and say these words:

Great Goddess, Mother of us all
Shine your light on me and send me your blessing
Fill me with your bright and vibrant energy
Let your radiance grant me calm and serenity
Wisdom, strength, and power
Help me find that radiance within my own self
And shine it back out into the world
In the best way possible
In your name, and with your guidance
So mote it be

Stand with the candle as long as feels right, absorbing the feeling of the night. If you want, you can leave the candle burning as long as it is safe to do so.

(

The full moon is also the perfect time to cleanse and clear your magical tools. While you don't have to do this every month, it's not a bad idea to do it periodically since they can pick up murky energy from their surroundings without you realizing. Crystals, especially, often absorb energy from their environment, which is part of what makes them so effective for healing work.

There are a number of different ways to cleanse your tools; you can place them under running water or sprinkle a mixture of water and salt on them (I don't recommend this for moisture-sensitive things like your Book of Shadows!) or waft them with cleansing herbs. But one of my favorite approaches is to place them in the light of the full moon overnight.

I find this is particularly effective with crystals, which seem to absorb the power of the moon and "recharge," but it can be used for any tool. It's also a good way to clear energy from a new tool, especially if it used to belong to someone else or if you're not sure of its origins. Try the spell below to see how it works for you.

• • • SPELL 5 • • •

Full Moon Tool Cleansing

In the best of all possible worlds, you would put the tools you wanted cleansed outside, where the moon could shine directly on them. Obviously, this isn't always going to be possible, whether because of your location, your living situation, the weather, or a dozen other reasons. Second best would be to leave them on a windowsill where the moonlight will hit them, but if even that won't work, simply putting them out on your altar or a table on the night of the full moon will work just fine.

You don't *need* to say a spell for this, but if you want to focus the lunar energy on your task, you can recite this simple one as you place the tool or tools where they will be for the night.

Sacred lunar light

Cleanse and clear this magical tool

Rid it of anything dark or dim

Fill it with your bright renewal

So mote it be

Because of its powerful energy and uniquely magical quality, the full moon is also a good time to work on your own personal empowerment and renewal. The world we live in can be demanding and challenging, and we rarely have enough opportunities to recharge our spiritual, emotional, and physical batteries. But when we don't take the time to do this, at least occasionally, we end

If you can only cast a spell on one night in a month, you might want to consider doing it on the full moon.

up exhausted and drained with nothing left in the tank to give to others or to ourselves.

The full moon is the perfect time to allow yourself the gift of being quiet and focusing on your own needs. Connecting with your identity as a witch can be a powerful thing and remind you of who and what you are. Channeling the energy of the full moon, which is often so potent that it keeps us awake, might just keep you going through the rest of the month until you can do it again.

· · · SPELL 6 · · ·
Full Moon Recharge

This spell can be done without any tools, or you can dress up in your magical attire (if you have it) and spread all your witchy tools around you. It's completely up to you. The most important thing is to remember to breathe deep and pull all that lunar energy deep inside, plugging into the full moon to recharge your spiritual batteries as much as you can.

Glorious full moon

Symbol of our Goddess

Night of magic and mystery

For those who follow the old ways

And those who create the new paths

Recharge and energize me

Fill me with your power and wonder

With every breath I take

Breathing in energy

Breathing in power

Breathing in serenity

Breathing in magic

To spark and inspire me

Through the rest of the month

Until your glorious orb fills the sky again

And fills my heart with magic

Breathe in and out slowly, feeling the moon's power for as long as feels right.

· · · ACTIVITY 11 · · ·

Planting a Moon Garden

If you are a gardener and have the space to do so, it can be fun to plant a full moon garden. There are a number of flowers that actually bloom at night, many of them white to match the moon, some of them blessed with spectacular scents.

Try planting the following flowers and then enjoy them on any evening, whether the moon is full or not: moonflower (a white climbing flower with a lemony aroma), evening primrose (pale pink and white), angel's trumpet (a white flower with a bell shape), night phlox, and evening stock.

New Moon

The new moon has a quieter energy than the full moon, which can often heighten emotions and make our animals bounce off the walls. (What, just at my house?) This makes it especially suited to magical work for new beginnings, or letting go of things that no longer work for us, or any spell we want to have tap into the waxing phase of the moon as it grows into the next full moon.

New moon spellcasting can be done outside (although there isn't much to see) or inside if that is more comfortable. We still invoke the Goddess, although we may call on her in her Maiden form rather than her Mother aspect, or invoke a darker goddess such as Hecate. New moon spells can be as simple or as complicated as you want, depending on the magical work you're doing and how this phase of the moon makes you feel.

··· Spell 7 ···

New Moon Beginnings

This spell is an example of how you can use the energy of the new moon to start something new. This may be a healthier lifestyle, or the first stirrings of a new relationship, or some new endeavor you'd like help or guidance with or a boost getting going on. (I might do this if I were starting to write a new book, for instance, just to get things off on the right foot.)

Start from seed or buy a small plant so that at the time of the spellcasting it is still little. Something that grows quickly would work best, but anything sturdy will do. The plant symbolizes the growth of whatever your goal is, so you will want to tend it carefully over the days to come. If you're not comfortable with plants, you can use a picture that represents whatever it is you're starting instead. Or both. A white candle is the only other thing you'll need. Place everything on your altar or table, light the candle, and spend a few minutes focusing on your goal before saying the spell.

Gentle Lady of the Moon
Smile down on me and send your blessing on my new beginning

Help me find the right ways to encourage its progress

Let it grow and be fruitful, and bring me rewards as I nurture it

And let it flourish with the waxing of the moon

So mote it be

New moons, especially the dark moon, the day on which the moon is not visible even as the smallest crescent, are good times for banishing or letting go of anything undesirable or unhelpful in your life. This can include unhealthy relationships or patterns or negative thoughts, among other things. It can also be debt, or illness, or other issues you want to get rid of.

Sometimes we do work on these types of things starting with the day after the full moon, as the moon enters its waning phase, so we can take advantage of the lunar energy for decrease. This spell can be used at either time.

· · · SPELL 8 · · ·

Banish the Negative

I like to use a black candle for this spell, but white will work just as well. If you want, you can use a picture or a symbol for whatever it is you wish to get rid of, or write it on a piece of paper if you can safely burn it when you're saying the spell. There is also a very cool type of paper that dissolves in water, which you can write things on if you can't use fire. (Find it online by searching for water-soluble paper.)

Light your candle and then either burn your paper using the candle and a firesafe bowl or dissolve if using the specialty paper. (Do this as you are saying the spell.) Alternatively, you can simply rip it into tiny pieces.

Diana, Goddess of Moonlight and Witches

Hear my call, and help me be free

Help me let go of things that no longer work

Of unhealthy habits and negativity

Banish the blues and darkness of thought

Rid me of those who don't wish me well

Aid me in releasing what I no longer need

With your bright blessing and this witch's spell

☽

If you are fortunate enough to find a familiar, it is nice to do a welcoming spell for your new magical companion. This can be done on the full moon, but it is also fine to do it at whatever phase of the moon it happens to be when your new member of the family joins you. Since you will be asking for the Goddess's blessing and introducing your familiar to her, a lunar spellcrafting is still very appropriate.

This is basically just an introduction and a welcoming spell, and a simple one at that, acknowledging your new friend.

· · · SPELL 9 · · ·
Welcoming a New Familiar

No candles for this one, unless you can be sure your familiar (be it cat, dog, ferret, or snake) won't get burned. Just stand with your familiar in front of your altar, or sit someplace where you can both be comfortable. Definitely don't bring them outside unless there is no chance they can run away. Don't worry, the Goddess will find you wherever you are.

Welcome, [name of animal]

Welcome to my home and my heart

Thank you for joining your life with mine

I welcome you to my home and to my magic

And promise to cherish and care for you

Goddess, meet [familiar's name]

[Familiar's name], meet the Goddess

> Whose blessings I ask upon you, and our work together
>
> Welcome, three times welcome
>
> To [familiar's name], my new familiar

Never force a familiar to do anything they aren't comfortable doing. It is enough simply to have their energy in the same space.

Chapter Six
SEASONAL SPELLS

As a nature-based religion, Witchcraft often focuses on tuning in to the varying energies of the changing seasons. The Wheel of the Year, as some people refer to it, is a series of eight sabbats, or holidays, spaced six weeks apart. It includes two solstices (summer and winter), two equinoxes (spring and fall), and four quarter-cross holidays that fall in between.

The solstices and equinoxes in particular have been celebrated for centuries in countries across the world, and various ancient cultures built sacred spaces that were believed to mark the movement of the sun. Stonehenge in England is one of the better-known examples.

Different cultures celebrated these holidays in different ways, and some of those practices have been adopted and adapted into modern observances you will likely find familiar. For instance, Imbolc, which falls on February 2 and celebrates the first subtle stirrings of life under the ground, evolved into Groundhog Day. The Winter Solstice, on or around December 21, lends many of its traditions to the modern Christian Christmas.

Regardless of cultural background, each of these holidays has a general theme that depends on its place in the seasonal cycle. Doing a spell that draws on the specific energy of that season can help you connect with nature and get the most benefit from the natural flow of the season.

These spells can be done with a formal ritual, including casting a circle, calling the quarters, invoking deity, and so on, or they can be kept fairly simple. It is just a matter of preference, although if you are sharing the sabbat with others, you might want to go for the full deal.

Unlike full moon spells, the sabbats usually invoke both Goddess and God, and there are often specific ones associated with each holiday, although that can vary depending on which pantheon or culture you follow, if any. I will sometimes suggest deities to call on for each sabbat, but feel free to use whichever gods you feel the most comfortable with, or simply use the nonspecific "God and Goddess."

The dates for the sabbats are usually noted for the Northern Hemisphere. If you live in the Southern Hemisphere, they will be reversed with the summer solstice falling in December and the winter one in June.

Imbolc—February 2

Imbolc celebrates the first subtle stirrings of spring, even if you live in a place where winter is still very much in control. It is a good reminder that the light is returning, and we too will soon need to come out of hibernation and return to a more active life. But don't be in a rush—this sabbat is the time to plan and prepare, not to jump into action. I like to use this holiday to set my goals, both magical and practical, for the year to come, and sometimes to ask for guidance on what those goals should be. Here is a spell that will help you do the same.

••• Spell 10 •••

Imbolc Goal Manifestation

Optional tools include a yellow candle on a firesafe plate or candleholder, a piece of paper on which to write your goals, a pen, and either a tarot or an oracle deck or a set of rune stones. The deity most commonly associated with Imbolc is Brigid, the Celtic goddess of smithcraft, creativity, and healing.

If you already know what your goals for the year are, write them down and place them under the candle. If you aren't sure or feel the need for some guidance, you can pull a card or two from the deck of your choice or pull out a rune stone first. Then light the candle and say this spell. (You can also say the spell and then do your divination, if that feels right to you.)

I call on Brigid, wise and creative

To shine her bright light on the year ahead

May she guide and inspire me

As I walk the path to achievement

May she help me stay focused

On my goals and priorities

Feed the fire of my spirit

And the passions of my heart

chapter six

And help me manifest success

In any and all positive ways

So mote it be

Spring Equinox—On or around March 21

The spring equinox, also known as Ostara, marks the beginning of spring and a time of rebirth and renewal. It has ties to Easter, which may or may not have gotten its name from the goddess Eostre (scholars aren't in agreement about this ... how unusual). At the equinox, we celebrate new beginnings, fertility (hence all the rabbits and chicks), and the return of light and energy to the land and to ourselves. It is also a good time to work on balance, since it is one of only two days in the year, the other being the autumn equinox, when the day and night are equal.

As you can see, this holiday has the potential to lend itself to many different types of magical work. I often use it to reinforce the goals I set for myself at Imbolc and send out renewed energy and intent to keep them moving forward. You can use the seeds you might well be planting anyway at this time of year to symbolize the potential for growth in your goals and in yourself. Even if you don't have a garden, you can put a small pot on a

windowsill or on your altar, or possibly a planter on a porch or balcony.

Spring Forward Movement

To do this spell, you will need a package of seeds, a small pot, some potting soil, and a small pitcher of water. Optional other items are a pen and paper to write your goals on, or a marker if you are using a pot you can write on, and, if you want, some small items to symbolize the goals you are working on.

Write your goals on the inside of your pot or on a piece of paper that you will stick inside the pot. Or simply visualize the things you wish to grow and flourish over the season ahead as you fill your pot with dirt and place a few seeds into the soil. If you want, you can name specific wishes with each seed. Take a moment to focus on all the things those seeds symbolize, then pour water slowly from your pitcher into the pot, a few drops at a time, while saying the spell.

Spring has come, bringing growth and potential

Along with the rains, soft or torrential

With each drop of water that's falling

Growth and success to me I am calling

With my will I nurture my dreams

All my hopes, and all my schemes

As each seed I gently sow

So my goals and plans will grow

· · · ACTIVITY 12 · · ·
Spiritual Spring-Cleaning

One simple way to integrate your magical life with your mundane life is to add a touch of Witchcraft to the most basic of tasks, like cooking or cleaning. Since many of us do some form of spring-cleaning anyway, it is easy to give your regular housecleaning a magical spin. As you sweep, visualize clearing away old, stagnant energy, or sweeping away negativity. You might want to mix up a special cleaning spray with a few essential oils that are good for purification (lemon, orange, or rosemary are all good for this), or even follow a more standard spring-cleaning by then sprinkling a mixture of salt and

> Negativity only feeds negativity, so whenever possible, send love out, even toward those who would harm you.

water through your home, or wafting the smoke from some cleansing herbs from room to room.

Beltane—May 1

Beltane, or May Day, is derived from an ancient Celtic fire festival that celebrates life, love, and fertility. In some areas, it was a time for fertility festivals that were aimed at helping crops grow. Beltane is a holiday full of passion and joyous abandon. Traditionally, people danced around the maypole, winding ribbons in and out to form a woven pattern that represented unity and the joining together of lovers and community.

If you can't have an actual maypole, tie ribbons on shrubbery outside or on a standing houseplant inside and dance around that. You can make a wish with every ribbon you tie.

Even if you have to celebrate the holiday on your own, you can still dance or celebrate love in whatever forms you would like it to manifest in your life.

• • • SPELL 12 • • •

Beltane Ribbon Revels

This simple spell can be done using anything from a small tree to a houseplant. All you need are a few colorful ribbons cut to about six- or eight-inch lengths. If you can do this outside, midday is a good time when the sun is strong above. If you have to be inside, you can always light a candle to represent the light of the sun.

If you want, you can even put on some music, or a recording of drumming, and dance as you tie your ribbons onto your "maypole," channeling your energy into the spell. You can call on any god or goddess associated with love, such as Venus, Aphrodite, Astarte, Eros, Cupid, or Aengus.

Keep in mind that you don't have to be asking for romantic love in the conventional sense. Celebrate any kind of love that appeals to you, from friends to pets to family.

> Ribbon bright and ribbon gay
> Grant my wish on Beltane's day
> Bring me love and passion true
> Grant me joy in all I do

Repeat with each ribbon you tie.

Summer Solstice—On or around June 21

The summer solstice, also known as Midsummer, is the longest day of the year, with the most light. The earth is bursting with energy and the sun is powerful. Cultures across the world have used this as a day of celebration and revelry, and my coven tends to do the same. In some places there are fire festivals to reflect the heat of the summer. In others there are pilgrimages to sacred waters for healing and vitality.

This is the perfect time to be outside if you can, usually during the day rather than the night. If you don't have any other witches to share your celebration, try inviting some open-minded friends over for a solstice picnic or barbeque. It's a good holiday to share with children, too, since this spell is easy and nonthreatening.

· · · SPELL 13 · · ·
Solstice Wishes

Even if you're on your own, you can embrace your own inner child and dance under the sunlit sky. The idea behind this spell is to draw on the abundant energy from below and above, and then use it to send your wishes out into the universe. While it is nice to have a bonfire if you can, all you really need for this is a bottle of bubbles.

Light your bonfire if you're having one, or simply stand outside under the sun. If you can be barefoot, that's great, but even if you're stuck inside with shoes on, this will work just fine. Feel the energy of the earth vibrating underneath your feet. Envision yourself as a great tree, with roots reaching down and pulling up all that power and potential. Then lift your arms to the sky and draw in the energy of the sun until you can feel yourself filled to the brim. Dance or chant if you are moved to do so. Then take your bottle of bubbles and blow your wishes, dreams, and desires out into the world, using the power of air that is your breath and fueling it with the summer's power. You can send out thank-yous too.

Air and water

Earth and sun

I celebrate

With joy and fun

Solstice day

So full and bright

Carry my wishes

Into the light

Lammas—August 1

Lammas, also known as Lughnasadh in honor of Lugh, the Celtic God of light, is the first of three Pagan harvest festivals in the Wheel of the Year. Specifically, it celebrates the grain harvest and is often observed with some form of bread. (Although cake is made from flour too, am I right?)

This first harvest festival is a good time to check in on your own personal harvests and see if you have achieved, or at least set into motion, the goals you wanted to harvest during this year. It is also an opportunity to refocus your attention if it has strayed, or change your path if the one you have been following isn't quite working for you.

A decorative broom is a great way to celebrate your witchy nature without anyone knowing.

· · · SPELL 14 · · ·
Focus and Potential

The following spell calls on Lugh and his power of light, as well as Demeter, the Greek goddess of the harvest, but you can simply say "God and Goddess" if you'd rather. It uses a loaf of rustic bread, preferably one with seeds and multiple grains, unless you can't eat that. (For those who are gluten intolerant, sourdough bread is often okay, but you can always substitute something else that represents the harvest instead of bread, like fruit or a vegetable.)

As you are saying the spell, think about all the energy that went into the grains, starting from a tiny seed and growing tall and strong through the summer until they could be harvested and turned into bread. Think too of all the work that went into the harvest—sowing the seeds, tending the crop, harvesting it, and then creating the bread. Your own goals and energy contain that same potential, and this spell is aimed at helping you achieve them.

Hold the bread up to the sky as you ponder this, then say the spell and take a few mindful bites.

Great Lugh and Sweet Demeter

I come to you on this harvest day

To ask for your aid with growth and prosperity

Help me focus on what is important

And spend my energy where it will do me the most good

So I might reach my fullest potential

And reap an abundant harvest from the seeds I have sown

Bless me with your light and love

So mote it be

Autumn Equinox—On or around September 21

The fall equinox, also known as Mabon, is the only day besides the spring equinox when the day and night are in perfect balance. It is the second harvest festival, and it is fitting to celebrate with the foods that are grown wherever you live. Where I am, that means fall fruits and vegetables like corn, squash, pumpkins, and apples, as well as cider. This day is sometimes referred to as the Witch's Thanksgiving because it is when we focus our attention on gratitude for the bounty of the earth.

From this point on, the Wheel turns toward darkness as we lose a little light every day. So it is even more important to celebrate what we have right now. This is a spell for gratitude and appreciation and a reminder that whether or not our harvests are as successful as we'd hoped, we still have everything we truly need.

· · · SPELL 15 · · ·

Gratitude

This spell is simple and can be used as part of a ritual or even at the start of a meal shared with friends. If you want, you can wait until dusk and say the spell as the sun is going down. Light a bonfire or a candle to symbolize the waning light or simply gaze at the stars as they appear in the sky. What's important is that you really focus on that feeling of gratitude and speak from the heart.

> I give thanks to the Universe
> For the bounty and gifts I have been given
> For the food on my table and the home where I live
> For friendship and family, whatever forms they take
> And for all the blessings present and yet to come
> I am grateful. I am blessed. I give thanks.

• • • ACTIVITY 13 • • •
Corn Dollies

Corn dolls are a traditional craft associated with Mabon. Not only do they celebrate corn, one of the grains of the season, but they can also be used to symbolize the sacrifice of the God for the good of the harvest, which was part of the mythology of many cultures.

Corn dollies are easy to make. You need the husks (outer leaves) from an ear of corn, something like cloth or rolled up paper to stuff the head, and some string or twine to tie it with. Optional: some people like to decorate their dolls with flowers or herbs. Take a couple of the largest leaves and fold them over the stuffing and tie it off to form the head. You will then have a skirt underneath. Take a smaller leaf or two and tie it across the body to form the arms. I find a figure eight winding of the twine helps secure the arms best. Then decorate if desired. Some people tuck a piece of paper inside the skirt and toss the dolly into a bonfire. Others hang it above their altar for the season.

Samhain—October 31

Samhain is considered by many to be the most witchy holiday of them all. Most people know it as Halloween (taken from the Christian holiday of All Hallows' Eve, which in turn was adapted from earlier Pagan origins), where ghosts and black cats and witches roam the night. Much of the modern lore is derived from the Pagan belief that on this night, the veil between the mundane world and the spirit world is at its thinnest.

On Samhain, because the veil between the worlds is thin, we often reach out to and celebrate those we have lost in the year gone by and in times before.

We use this time to do divination, speak to our loved ones who have passed on, and generally celebrate all that is witchy and magical. Samhain can be a wonderful night to get together with other witches, if this option is available to you. But even if you are on your own, you can take comfort from knowing that all across the world, many witches are celebrating their magical nature along with you.

Samhain is considered by many to be the Witch's New Year, and we can use this time to let go of the year behind us and welcome in the year to come. We often call on the darker gods and Crone goddesses, or those who are connected with the wilder side of nature. (I use Hecate and the Horned God here, but feel free to substitute any others you prefer.)

• • • SPELL 16 • • •
Wonderfully Witchy

This spell celebrates the witchy nature of the sabbat and encourages you to embrace your own inner witch in all its power and glory. On this night of all nights, be proud to be a witch!

If you can be outside around a bonfire, that's great. But it can also be just as wonderful to put some drumming or Pagan music on in the background and dance around your living room. Find a chant you like and repeat it over and over until you can feel it resonate in your bones. Or if quiet is more your thing, simply light a black candle in a firesafe container and recite the spell with all your energy and focus behind it.

Hail to the Horned God!

Hail to Hecate!

It is Samhain and magic reigns

It is Samhain and the veil thins

But I am not afraid of the darkness

Nor do I shy away from the light

I am a witch and I will dance

And drum, and chant

I acknowledge the ancestors and their gifts

I worship the Old Gods and learn from the past

I embrace my own power and walk my own path

Witchy and wild

Magical and wonderful

I am a witch and I will sing

The song of my people

Hear me! Hear me! Hear me!

I am magic and tonight is my night

Winter Solstice—On or around December 21

The winter solstice, also known as Yule, is the longest night of the year. In cultures around the world, people celebrate the returning of the light, because after this, the days begin slowly to grow longer, just a few minutes at a time, until finally the warmth returns with the spring.

Like its opposite, the summer solstice, the winter solstice has been celebrated all across the globe. In addition, its traditions were adapted almost entirely into the Christian holiday of Christmas, including the use of cut pine trees decorated for the season (which represent life in the midst of the death of winter), caroling (taken from the tradition of "going wassailing," where people went from house to house singing and being given drinks), the use of holly and mistletoe, and more.

Many Christmas carols refer to Yule in lines such as "celebrate the Yuletide merry." Yule is a synonym for Christmas and has been for centuries, but it originally was the name of a heathen feast.

The nice thing about all this is that it makes the winter solstice an easy holiday to share with others, even if they don't identify as witches. You can have a winter solstice feast and exchange presents, and people will feel right

A WINTER
SOLSTICE FEAST

Because of the way the Yule traditions have been taken over and integrated with modern practices, this can be the perfect opportunity to share your witchy beliefs with others in a playful and non-threatening way.

You can start by throwing a winter solstice or Yule dinner party and serving seasonal foods. (A potluck is great, because then you're not stuck with all the cooking.) If you want, you can discuss some of the elements of a winter solstice celebration. Your guests will probably be amazed to learn how much of Christmas started with Pagan customs! Have everyone light a candle to celebrate the returning of the sun.

at home. If you have a particularly open-minded group of friends or family, you can even try reciting this spell together in celebration of the returning of the light.

••• Spell 17 •••
The Light Returns

Whether you do it with others or by yourself, it is traditional to turn off all the lights in the house and then go from room to room lighting candles to symbolize the returning sun. You can do this if it is safe to do so, or you can simply turn the lights in the room you are in down or off and light a number of small candles (tea lights on a pottery plate work well) as you say the spell.

Winter solstice blessings

As we greet the sun's return

In the midst of darkness

These small candles do we burn

To symbolize the light above

And the light inside

We greet the sun's returning

Arms and hearts, we open wide

All hail the sun's return!

Chapter Seven

SPELLS FOR LOVE, FRIENDSHIP, AND JOY

Love spells may be one of the most popular types of magical work. But love comes in many forms, and you can also do spells for friendship and for joy in general. Those are all pretty magical things, after all.

The spells in this chapter are just the tip of the iceberg, but they should give you a place to start and maybe even some ideas for spells of your own.

Even though love spells may be common, I think they are also one of the trickiest kinds of spells to get right.

It can be tempting to cast a spell to make someone love you, but I always suggest that instead you do magic to open yourself to love and trust that the gods or the universe will send you the person who is right for you. We can't always see clearly when the heart is involved, and it is better to leave the door open for options you might not perceive from the place you're standing.

• • • SPELL 18 • • •
Love Is Light

This spell is more "send me the love I need" than "send me the love I want." That way, if romantic love isn't in the cards right now, you might still get some form of love to fill the lonely spaces. Or maybe, just maybe, the love that shows up will be exactly what you wanted but didn't know to ask for. Try to keep an open mind and an open heart and see what happens.

To do this spell, you can use some lavender flowers or rose petals (dried or fresh), a pink candle (red if you want passionate love), and a piece of amethyst or rose quartz. If you want to take things one step further, you can etch a heart into the candle and/or write your name on it with a toothpick, fingernail, or athame. You can also wrap a piece of pink or red ribbon around the base of the candle, making sure it doesn't get near the flame.

Place the candle on a firesafe plate and sprinkle the herbs around it if you're using them. You can rub the flowers between your hands and inhale the scent to really feel their power. Hold on to the stone and light the candle, then recite the spell. If you want, you can carry the stone with you for a while or place it on your altar or under your pillow.

Aphrodite, Isis, Inanna

Goddesses of love so bright

Send me what it is I need

Light as love, love as light

Grant me love to make me happy

To fill my heart and so my spirit

Love that fits me like a glove

And warms me when I am near it

Give to me the love I'm missing

Send to me the love that's right

I trust in your divine wisdom

Light as love, and love as light

Love comes into our lives in many variations, and in addition to romantic love and love of family, one of the most important forms is the love of friends. For some people, there may not be a significant other (maybe they don't even want one, or maybe they do but the right person still hasn't come along), and for many, family can be problematic.

Friends can become the family we choose. That is certainly the case with the women in my coven, who have been (most of us) practicing together for twenty years and have been there for all the big ups and downs.

> When working with love magic, remember that love takes many forms and isn't limited to the romantic.

· · · SPELL 19 · · ·

Friendship Bracelet

If you want to draw in a new friend or strengthen the friendships you already have, you can try doing this spell. Remember that you are not casting this on someone in particular—just putting it out into the universe with an open heart. You can light a white or pink candle, and if you want something extra on the altar, a piece of rose quartz (which you can carry with you later) is a nice addition. If you want an actual bracelet to wear to help draw friendship to you, you can make one from beads like rose quartz or aventurine or amethyst or pick a favorite you already own and charge that with the energy of this spell.

Friendship is a blessing

A gift from an open heart

Troubles shared are troubles halved

And where solutions start

Someone to be by my side

Through the good and bad

Friendship strong and friendship wise

With one whose heart is glad

Send me friendship bright and new

And strengthen those that waver

So next to friends tried and true

Life's moments I will savor

Life can be hectic and overwhelming, and even when things are good, we can forget to take time out to truly embrace the moments of joy when they come along. This next spell is a reminder and encouragement to do just that.

Embrace Joy

You can say this spell without any extra tools, but if you want to create a joy altar, try decorating it with pictures or items that symbolize the things that bring you joy, like a shell from the ocean or a photo of a favorite vacation spot or activity. Take a few minutes before saying the spell to focus on some of your best memories or dreams of things you would like to do.

> I open my arms and open my heart
> To all of life's great pleasures
> Allowing joy to fill my cup
> With small and mighty treasures
> I'll not forget to pay attention
> When wonders come along
> Embracing joy that life imparts
> And singing every song

Sometimes one of the most difficult types of love to achieve is self-love. For most of us, it is easier to accept the flaws and imperfections of those around us than it is to accept them in ourselves.

We may look in the mirror and see ugliness where others find beauty. If only we could be as kind to ourselves as we are to others; think how much happier we would be.

It is hard to have reasonable expectations for ourselves (especially if you happened to have been raised by critical or demanding parents, or spent time in relationships with a significant other who put you down), but that makes it even more important to strive to give ourselves the love and unconditional acceptance we give the others we value. Remind yourself that the Goddess loves all her children, and then say this spell.

· · · SPELL 21 · · ·

Self-Love

Use a hand mirror if you have one or stand in front of a mirror in your house. If you have to, you can use the photo app on your phone to look at yourself (although I usually suggest keeping technology out of magical work) or find a photo of yourself you like.

You can dress up if you want, put on makeup if you use it, or wear a piece of magical jewelry that makes you feel powerful. Or you can do this in your jammies, if that's what makes you the most comfortable. Just be you. If you want, you can use a pink or white candle and do the spell in its dim flickering light. For a touchstone to remind you to practice self-love, it is nice to have a chunk of amethyst or rose quartz somewhere you'll see it or will pass often. If you're using one, hold it while you say the spell.

Great Goddess, who loves us all

Help me love myself

Help me see the good that others see in me

And listen only to the voices that speak with caring

Aid me in letting go of old patterns

That stand in the way of seeing my own worth

And beauty and wisdom and strength

Let me see myself as you see me

Imperfect, perhaps, but still deserving of love

And help me learn to love myself

Today and always

Deity lives in us all

A tiny fragment of the greater whole

So I too am divine and worthy of love

I love myself

I accept myself

Today and always

Spend a few more minutes looking at yourself and let the feeling of self-love settle in. Do this as often as you need to, especially if you are struggling with the shift in the beginning.

Chapter Eight
SPELLS FOR PROSPERITY AND SUCCESS

After love spells, the next most commonly performed magical work is for prosperity and success. Who among us couldn't occasionally use a little help with money issues, or getting the job we want, or having some important event go well? There are some folks who believe it is a misuse of magic to use it for monetary gain, but I think that as long as you aren't doing anything to harm anyone else and you keep your requests reasonable, there's no reason why you shouldn't use all the tools you have to achieve what's important to you.

For instance, I spent many years making and selling gemstone jewelry. I would often do prosperity magic before a major craft show with the intent of having everything go as well as possible. I was simply reinforcing the hard work I was already doing with a little magical boost of energy.

That's the important thing to remember about spells for prosperity and success. You can cast a spell, but you also need to put in the effort and follow through with actions afterward. You also want to leave an opening for the universe to grant your wish in ways you might not have anticipated. You never know what will happen.

• • • Spell 22 • • •

Prosperity

The following is a spell for general prosperity. You can use it anytime your finances need some help or if you're stressing over money. Optional tools include a green candle, any green stone (like aventurine, malachite, or jade), and some basil, peppermint, or cinnamon. If you want to combine this spell with a prosperity charm bag, there are instructions for one right afterward.

Great Goddess, great God

Grant me prosperity

In any and all positive ways

To pay my bills and reduce my debt

Open doors and send opportunities

Let abundance flow forth

From all my efforts and hard work

For the good of all

So mote it be

If you want to make a focus for this spell, you can create a charm bag with some of the spell elements and hold it while saying the spell. Then you can carry the bag with you, especially if you are dealing with money matters, or put it on your altar. To give it an extra boost, anoint the bag with magical money-drawing oil. Money-drawing oil is a magical oil made up of various essential oils from herbs associated with prosperity, combined and then consecrated for that purpose.

It is always okay to ask for help when you need it, whether from the gods or from others.

• • • Activity 14 • • •

Prosperity Charm Bag

To make this bag, you will need the following: a small drawstring bag or a piece of fabric and yarn or ribbon to tie it closed with, a piece of tumbled aventurine or malachite or jade or tiger's eye, a few dried herbs (I like to use basil, peppermint, and a stick of cinnamon, but there are plenty to choose from), and a coin (I like something special like a half-dollar or dollar coin, but anything will do as long as it is shiny and nice looking).

Place all your ingredients in the bag or in the middle of the cloth. Do this slowly and mindfully, focusing on your intention to bring more prosperity and abundance into your life. Pull the bag closed or tie off the fabric with your ribbon to make it into a bag. Then say the previous spell.

☾

Abundance can mean different things to different people, but it isn't necessarily the same thing as prosperity. Prosperity is more focused on money, whereas abundance is more about having the basic things you need in amounts that mean you don't have to worry about them.

Abundance can be an overflowing garden to help you feed your family, or enough time and energy to get things done, or gifts from unexpected places just when you need them.

Abundance

This spell is very simple and only asks that your life be filled with whatever it is you need to feel secure and relaxed about the future.

If you want, you can light a green or white candle. As you say the spell, try to visualize whatever it is that abundance means to you.

> Let my life be full and nourishing
> Overflowing with all I need
> Growth and plenty, always flourishing
> Abundance now is mine indeed

(

Along with spells for prosperity and abundance, we also have spells for success. Sometimes those things overlap, but success can mean different things to different people and may change depending on the situations you're dealing with.

For instance, if you have a part in a play, success may mean getting through all your performances without

Focus
ON THE POSITIVE

When you are doing work for prosperity, abundance, or success, it is important to maintain a positive attitude, no matter how dire the situation might be. I realize that this may be easier said than done, but I have found that starting with the belief that everything is going to work out okay usually means it does.

This is where faith comes in. Faith in the gods, in your own magic, and in your ability to make positive changes. It may not all happen exactly how you expect or want it to, but sometimes that just opens the door for something even better. If you get the help you need, don't forget to say thank you!

messing up your lines and having the audience like your performance. Or you may have a meeting or a date that you want to go well. None of those things have anything to do with prosperity, although there may be times when succeeding at something (like getting a great new job) can lead to that.

When you are doing a spell for success, you want to have a clear idea of what that means at that particular time, but of course you can use the same spell on different occasions for different goals.

• • • SPELL 24 • • •
Success

For this spell, you will need something that symbolizes whatever it is you want to succeed at (so, if you were in a play, you might want your script or a picture of the stage, and if you are going on a date, you might use a heart-shaped stone or a picture of a couple eating together), or you can write it down on a piece of paper if you can't find anything suitable. This is to help you focus on your goal. You can use a green candle, but you can also change the candle color to be appropriate for whatever you wish to succeed at, like yellow for intellect if you want to do well on a test, or red for something you're passionate about.

For extra oomph, you can etch *success* or a word or two to represent your goal into the candle. I also like the runes Tir, Uraz, and Gifu for success work. Light the candle and say the spell.

I will succeed at this task

To which I give my all

For their help the gods I ask

That fate answers my call

Success is mine, so I know

I have the faith and will

For my efforts success shall show

And my wishes now fulfill

You can do the spell the day before a big event or on a continual basis if the goal is something ongoing.

Chapter Nine
SPELLS FOR HEALING AND PEACE

It is all very well and good to have love and prosperity, but if you don't have health, you probably will have a tough time enjoying the good things in your life. Of course, the word *health* covers a broad scope: there is physical health, mental health, even spiritual health. Thankfully, you can do spells for whatever your issues are.

Health is also one of those areas where it is occasionally okay to do a spell on someone else's behalf as long as you have gotten their permission ahead of time. When one of our coven members is having surgery (or giving birth, for that matter), we have all gathered to do a spell for success and fast healing. It can be very rewarding to help someone heal.

But primarily, like all other spells, healing work is done for ourselves. It can be challenging to find the focus and energy to do complicated spellcrafting when you're not feeling your best, so feel free to keep these spells simple. You can always make a healing poppet (in the section on tools earlier in this book) or a charm bag. Magical oils can be helpful too. But sometimes you just want to light a candle, hold a crystal, and maybe drink a cup of tea made from healing herbs, and that's okay too.

If you are dealing with a chronic health problem or ongoing issue, you may want to say a spell for the first time on the full moon, using whatever tools or extra aids to focus your power. Then repeat the spell every night for a week or even a month. If you want to really go with the flow of lunar energy, try doing a spell to increase health during the waxing moon (from the new moon until the full moon), then change over to a spell to decrease illness for the second half of the lunar cycle (from the day after the full moon until the new moon comes around again).

SPELLS FOR OTHERS

There is nothing wrong with doing magical work to help someone else as long as you have their permission first. You might think that since you are doing a good thing, there is no reason to ask, but not everyone would be happy to have a spell said for them.

For one thing, folks from other religious paths may not approve of Witchcraft, even when its intentions are positive. For another, especially when you are dealing with some form of illness, there may be reasons for that person to be sick that you can't understand. Perhaps there are lessons they need to learn from the challenges. Or they need to take actions to heal themselves.

Either way, it is never appropriate to do a spell that affects another person unless you have okayed it with them first.

Healing for Body and Spirit

The following spell can be used at any time and repeated
as often as needed. If you want to make it easy and simple,
just light a blue or white candle and recite
the spell. For a little more oomph, you
can carve healing runes and any symbols
that appeal to you into the candle and add
a healing herb or herbs—such as calendula,
dill, lavender, rosemary, and/or lemon balm—
plus an appropriate stone like crystal quartz, amethyst,
bloodstone, or turquoise.

I call on the gods of healing

Apollo and Belenus, Brigid and Eir

Isis, Kwan Yin, and Rhiannon

Send me your gifts of healing

Gentle and loving and kind

That I might be healed in body and spirit

Healed in heart and mind

Growing stronger every day

Healed with your loving power

From this day forward

So mote it be

chapter nine

Even if we are physically healthy, many of us struggle to find peace and serenity in an often challenging world. There are practical ways to address this: turn off the news, practice meditation or Tai Chi, seek out the positive. Pet a cat. Or five. But even when we do our best to stay calm and centered, inner peace can sometimes be hard to attain. This spell may help give a boost to the rest of your efforts.

••• SPELL 26 •••
Peace and Serenity

Optional extra tools that work especially well with this type of magical work are herbs like lavender, chamomile, rose, and lemon balm and stones like crystal quartz, amethyst, and rose quartz. You might also want to focus on a picture of something you find calming and soothing. For me, that's the ocean, but for you that might be a meadow full of flowers, a majestic tree, a sunset, or a pile of cute puppies or kittens. Whatever works for you. I like to use a plain white candle, but yellow, light blue, or lavender is also good.

God and Goddess

Please grant me peace

Soothe my spirit and calm my mind

Replace chaos with clarity

And help me find my way

To peace and serenity

[Take a deep breath]

I breathe in peace

[Take a deep breath]

I breathe in calm

[Take a deep breath]

I breathe in serenity

[Take a deep breath]

Ahhhhhhhhhhh

Hold your hands in front of your heart, holding the stone if using one, and just spend a few minutes sitting quietly.

Along with healing and peace, there are times when we could all use a little extra strength. Whether we are facing a particularly difficult challenge or just feeling overwhelmed by the massive amount of things we have on our plates (yes, this is the voice of experience), we all hit a point where life asks more from us than we have left in the tank.

• • • SPELL 27 • • •
Strength from Within and Without

This spell works both by asking the universe to send you extra strength and by helping you tap into your own inner core of power you might not even realize is there. You can charge a crystal or stone to carry around with you, or a favorite necklace to wear as a reminder. Or simply hold your hands over your core (near your belly button) and channel the energy inside so you can draw on it during moments of need.

Goddess, give me strength

To do the things I need to do

To be there for myself and others

To stand strong in the face of adversity

And find the allies I need when I need them

Goddess, send me energy

Willpower and courage

Remind me to believe in myself

As you believe in me

Goddess, send me strength

So mote it be

☾

Physical health is the most obvious type of healing that most people ask for, but mental health is just as important. Even if your body is strong and vibrant, you can still struggle with depression, anxiety, PTSD, and numerous other mental health issues that impact your life and interfere with your ability to function well or enjoy the good things that surround you.

Serious mental health issues should always be dealt with by professionals, whether these are doctors, counselors, or both. But while you are doing whatever is necessary for self-care with a more traditional approach, you can also add in a spiritual component. In addition to whatever other spiritual practices you find helpful, you can also try saying this spell.

> Sometimes courage means doing something not because you aren't afraid, but despite it.

• • • SPELL 28 • • •
Mental Health

All you need is a white candle and a quiet space. And in times of need, you can do without the candle.

Great Goddess, great God

I ask that you help me with my mental health

Heal my spirit and my heart

Let my mind and nerves be calm

Let my thoughts be rational and reasonable

Let my emotions be soothed and uplifted

Help me achieve a state of balance and health

In mind and body and spirit

So mote it be

Chapter Ten

SPELLS FOR PROTECTION AND PURIFICATION

Let's face it—we live in a dangerous world. Some of the dangers we can do our best to avoid by locking our doors and driving carefully or getting vaccines, but no matter how cautious we are, there is a lot of bad stuff (and some bad people) out there. So in addition to taking all the practical steps we can to keep ourselves and our loved ones and our possessions safe, it never hurts to add a little magical work on top.

There are many different forms of protection magic. There are spells for safe travels, spells to thwart thieves, spells against those with malicious intent toward you or your home. In my book *The Little Book of Cat Magic*, I even have a spell to keep your cat safe if they go outside (although I really don't recommend that under most circumstances).

The first thing you want to do is figure out exactly what kind of protection you want, and then find or write the spell that suits your needs. If you are sending your child off to college on their own for the first time, you will probably want a different spell than one you'd use to protect your car.

Some tools, like a magical protection oil, can be used for multiple applications. For instance, you can do a spell on your kid and anoint them with the oil, if they'll let you, and use the same oil to bless your vehicle. Other magical paraphernalia—such as charm bags, inscribed candles, or even the witch bottle from earlier in the book—work best for specific situations and won't really apply in others. Once you figure out what kind of protection magic you want to do, you can decide from there which tools, if any, you want to use with your spell.

I do yearly protection magic on my home and all those who live in it. Because I live in the snowy northeast, I renew it every fall before winter sets in. If you live in a place with dangerous storms, you might want to do it right before tornado or hurricane season. Or if you live in a bad neighborhood, you might even want to do it once a month. There's no wrong way.

Because I have a house in the country, I make up an herbal protection mix and sprinkle it around the outside of the house and along the front boundaries of my property, paying special attention to the end of the driveway and the mailbox where things and people come in from the outside world. If you live in an apartment, you will probably have to do the spell on the inside of your home, so you might want to use less salt and fewer herbs or simply vacuum them up after they've had a few hours or a day to sit.

Alternatively, you can make up a simple protection spray and spritz it around the inside of your home. If you do that, make sure you use herbs whose smell you like!

Protection Herbal Mixture and Spray

The herbal mixture that I use is very simple. I put all the ingredients together in a jar and stir them up, then sprinkle them around as I walk the edges of my house and property and recite the simple spell over and over. (I keep the spell simple so I can remember it and not have to hold a piece of paper at the same time.)

I use sea salt, dried basil, dill, garlic, and rosemary. If you're going to use this inside, you might want to leave out the garlic. Other good protection herbs to add or substitute include chamomile, juniper, parsley, and sage. I mash my mixture together in a mortar and pestle I reserve for magical work, but you can just crumble the herbs up and mix them with your fingers if you prefer. For a little extra oomph, you can put a tumbled piece of red jasper or black onyx in the jar and let it sit for a day.

To make a protection room spray instead, use the essential oils of three or more of the herbs and mix them with water and a few drops of alcohol in a spray bottle. Then spritz it around in each room, taking special care with doors, windows, and any other places where things come in, even chimneys.

Protection for Home and Self

Try saying this spell while using your protection mix or spray, or simply visualize a protective white light surrounding your home.

This house is protected

This home is protected

This place is protected

From any dangers from without or within

Accidental or intentional

From nature and human malice

This house is protected

All those who live within it are protected

This place is protected

Repeat until you have gone over the entire area.

(

Purification is another way to keep yourself safe, healthy, and functioning at your best. We all pick up nasty energy from the world around us, most of it unintentional, although occasionally malice is aimed at us specifically. I'm not necessarily talking about hexing or people casting evil spells on you—that happens, but not as often as you'd think. But when folks are angry or resentful, some of that emotion can stick to you unless you have very good psychic barriers.

Plus, there are our own unpleasant thoughts and feelings, which can leave us feeling murky and drained. It's not a bad idea to do some form of purification work from time to time in order to rid ourselves of whatever negative energy we're carrying around. You can integrate this into a simple ritual in your daily shower, but sometimes you need something with a little more power. For those occasions, you can use this spell.

· · · SPELL 30 · · ·
Purification

All you need for this spell is a white candle (the biggest candle you have, because you want it to shine a bright light if possible), a bowl, a pitcher of water, a small bowl with salt, and some form of cleansing herbs or incense. Make sure you have a holder to put your herbs or incense in.

Light the candle and take a minute to focus on the flame. Then slowly and mindfully pour the water into the bowl, followed by a little salt, which you can mix with your finger or an athame. As you say the spell, first cup your hand over the candle (being careful not to get too close to the flame) and bring that hand up over the top of your head and then down your body in a sweeping motion.

SAY: With the power of Fire, I purify and cleanse my body and spirit.

Dip your fingers into the bowl of salt and water and anoint yourself on your crown (top of the head), third eye (middle of the forehead), throat, heart, solar plexus (belly), sacral, and root chakras.

SAY: With the power of Earth and Water, I purify and cleanse my body and spirit.

Light your purifying herbs or incense and waft it from head to toe.

SAY: With the power of Air, I purify and cleanse my body and spirit.

Let the herbs smolder in the holder for a few minutes as you breathe in and out and visualize yourself encompassed in glowing golden light. When you're ready,

SAY: I am cleansed and purified. So mote it be.

Blow out the candle and snuff out the herbs.

EASY PURIFICATION TECHNIQUES

Sometimes you need a little cleansing but don't have time for a full spellcasting. Try any of these simple techniques for something fast and easy.

- While taking a shower, focus on washing away anything that doesn't benefit you. You can literally wash it out of your hair.
- On the night of the full moon, go outside and visualize the light from the moon coming down in magical rays to purify your body and spirit with the Goddess's love.
- Keep a bowl of water by the entrance to your home and dip your hand into it whenever you come in from outside, concentrating on letting all the "gunk" from the outside world slide off you and into the water.
- Stand in front of your altar or in a quiet space. Visualize your body being surrounded by a glowing white or yellow light. Feel it washing over and through you, cleansing and purifying.

On rare occasions, protection and purification magic aren't enough to keep negative energies away, especially if they are being sent in your direction by someone who intends to harm you. As I said, this is more unusual than people think, but if you are certain there is someone (magical or otherwise) who is wishing you ill, you can do a binding spell.

• • • Spell 31 • • •
Binding

This is serious magic and not to be done lightly, since it can be difficult to undo if you change your mind or find out you were mistaken. This spell is written to try to avoid unintentional harm, but it should still be used only when absolutely necessary.

For this, you will need a length of black yarn, ribbon, or thread, a piece of paper and a pen, and a black candle. (White will do if that is all you have. Simply tie another piece of black thread or yarn at the very base of the candle.) You can also use a small box or container if you want.

Light the candle. Write the name of the person who is trying to harm you or you believe is sending malicious energy toward you on the piece of paper and roll it up into a scroll shape. As you are saying your spell, tie the piece of black yarn or ribbon around the paper and tie it with nine knots. For extra protection, you can drip a few drops of wax from your candle on the knots and/or put the roll into a box and tie another length of black yarn or thread around that.

Try to do all this calmly and without anger. You don't want to put more negativity into the situation; you simply want to keep this person from harming you further.

I bind you, [name of person]

From causing harm toward me or mine

From sending ill in my direction

I bind you now with good intent

In the cause of my own protection

I bind you, [name of person]

[repeat nine times as you tie your knots]

You are bound and can harm no more

You are bound with love

I turn the key and lock the door

So mote it be

Chapter Eleven

SPELLS FOR DIVINATION AND POWER

There are many aspects to Witchcraft that may or may not come naturally to you. For instance, divination is something that is easier for some people than it is for others, but that doesn't mean you can't learn how to do it. Sometimes it is a matter of finding the form of divination that works best for you. Some people are drawn to tarot cards, others like rune stones, still others simply open their minds and gaze into a dark scrying surface.

In fact, Witchcraft in general can be said to consist of part instinct, part innate talent, and (a large part) practice. Some witches may seem to be unusually powerful, but for most of us, that power comes from a combination of faith and repetition, something anyone can attain. There is a reason we call it the Craft, since like most arts, it takes patience and a willingness to learn and grow.

These spells are a way to get in touch with your own instinctive gifts and also a form of magical exercise that will help you flex your spiritual muscles and get stronger in your own witchy way.

For some witches, divination comes easily and may have been part of their path before they even discovered Witchcraft. For others, it seems difficult and unattainable. Most folks fall somewhere in the middle, intrigued but not quite sure how to make it part of their regular practice.

· · · Spell 32 · · ·
All-Purpose Divination

No matter where you are on that sliding scale, you can say this spell before doing any form of divination to help you tune in and feel more confident. Hold on to whatever you are using (tarot cards, oracle cards, runes stones, pendulum, whatever) and say this spell. You can do it once or use it every time you sit down to do any kind of divination.

God and Goddess, shine your light on me

Let my eyes see clearly

Let my mind be open

And my intuition be strong

Guide me as I look beyond this moment

And into what was, is, and might become

Give me the answers I seek

And show me what I need to see

So mote it be

A lot of witches are drawn to tarot and oracle cards in particular. There are so many different varieties that there is something to appeal to almost everyone. Some people find tarot cards a little overwhelming and like oracle cards, which have less of a learning curve. Either way, this is definitely one of those cases where practice can really increase both your comfort level and your skill.

I find it can be helpful to pull one card every day from whichever deck or decks you use, both for the practice and to get more in tune with your own deck. (They really do develop a feel for you, just as you are developing a feel for them.)

• • • SPELL 33 • • •
Card Reading Charm

This very simple spell is one you can recite to boost a card reading. Hold on to whatever cards you are using as you say it.

> I am one with the cards
>
> And they are one with me
>
> Let us work together
>
> And see what we will see

Power means different things to different people, especially when you are talking about magical work. Maybe it is the ability to cast a spell and have it do what you want it to, at least most of the time. Maybe it is a level of confidence in your own strength and the knowledge that no matter what life throws at you, you are capable of not only surviving, but thriving.

Being a powerful witch doesn't necessarily mean that you can control people and events around you, but it can mean that you have the tools you need to make the most out of whatever situation you find yourself in. Mostly it is a matter of feeling empowered, which in turn lends more power to your magical work.

· · · SPELL 34 · · ·
Power Push

For this spell, you can use a piece of carnelian or amethyst or crystal quartz. (A necklace with one or more of those stones will work well if you want to be able to feel empowered in public situations, otherwise a tumbled stone or crystal for your altar is fine.) An orange or red candle is great if you have one, but white is always fine. To really add some oomph to the spell, you can use a little cinnamon essential oil on the candle or rub some dried cinnamon near the bottom of the candle.

After you say the spell, you can carry your stone with you, put it on your altar, or even stick it under your pillow. When you feel like you need to recharge it—or yourself— simply say the spell again.

The quickest way to lose your magical power is to abuse it.

Light the candle, hold the stone in your hand, and say the spell. Focus on feeling powerful, empowered, and witchy.

I am a witch

And I am powerful

I am grounded like the Earth

Flexible like the Water

Subtle like the Air

Glowing like the Fire

The God and Goddess are within me

And without, always there

I am a witch

My power comes from inside

Deep in the core of who I am

No one can take it from me

And it grows stronger every day

I am a witch

And I am power personified

Chapter Twelve

Spells for Grounding and Courage

I t can be hard to stay grounded in the chaotic world we live in, especially if your life is overwhelming due to the demands of work and the needs of other people. Let's face it, staying grounded is hard no matter what. But when your head and heart are all over the place, it can be hard to focus enough to do anything well, including magical work.

There are plenty of practical everyday things you can do to ground yourself: spend time in nature or out in the garden, do Yoga or Tai Chi or take a walk, meditate, cook mindfully, and so on. But if you don't have the time or inclination to do those kinds of activities or simply can't get to them as often as you'd like to, you can do this grounding spell too.

• • • Spell 35 • • •
Grounding

If possible, it is wonderful to do this spell sitting outside on the ground, or under a tree, or (if you're really lucky) by the ocean or some other body of water. But any quiet spot will work. You can either sit on the floor or ground or stand or sit with your feet firmly planted.

You don't need any tools for this, just your focus and the intention to become more grounded. As you say the spell, visualize yourself drawing energy from the land underneath you and strengthening your natural connection with the earth.

> I reach down to the earth below
>
> Sending down roots
>
> Pulling up energy
>
> Feeling its solid strength
>
> Becoming part of me

With every deep breath in

And deep breath out

I am grounded

I am grounded

I am grounded

☾

I find grounding to be so important in today's world, and so difficult to achieve, that I am including a second spell with that goal. This one is a little different in that it is a mix of grounding and calming, so you might find it helpful to do after a rough day, or an unsettling argument, or even just after watching the news when something dramatic and upsetting has occurred. (So any day, really.)

• • • SPELL 36 • • •
Calm and Ground

I like to light a candle and watch the flame for a while, maybe with calming music or ocean sounds in the background, then say the spell and simply sit for as long as I can spare, breathing in and out slowly until I can feel the tension seep out of my body.

I am calm like the ocean on a quiet day

Or the gentle spatter of rain on the flowers

I am grounded like the earth below my feet

Solid and steady as a stone

I am softly glowing like the embers of a bonfire

Lit from within by my own sacred flame

I am the gentle wind, that blows away cobwebs and confusion

And brings the scents of nature to calm and soothe

I am calm and grounded

I am at peace

Another issue that can get in the way of our best functioning is fear. This isn't to say that it's not normal to be afraid of things. We all have our triggers, and most of them are fairly realistic. But sometimes fear takes over or gets in the way of our accomplishing important aspects of our lives. Then you might want to consider doing a spell for courage.

If you're afraid of flying, for instance, you could do the spell before a trip. If you are afraid of public speaking and have to talk at an important event, this spell might help make you more comfortable. Carnelian is my favorite

If you can only have one large stone, clear crystal quartz is powerful and versatile.

stone to use for courage work, although turquoise and hematite work well for some people, so you can use whichever one feels best to you. You only need a small piece, something you can stick in your pocket and touch if you need a reminder of the spell.

· · · SPELL 37 · · ·

Courage

This spell is simple, so you can whisper it under your breath later on if you need to. Just place the stone you're using in front of a white or orange candle, light the candle, and focus on the energy for courage being absorbed by both the stone and your heart.

God and Goddess

Lend me courage

Keep me strong

Despite my fears

Courage today

Courage tomorrow

Courage to last

Through all the years

I am not afraid

So mote it be

chapter twelve

One final area of our lives that most of us could use a little extra help with is balance. Very few of us (including me) can say we have a good balance between work and play, time with others and time for ourselves, giving and receiving, and, of course, our mundane lives and our spiritual lives. If you're like most people, you probably spend too much time working, have more unhealthy habits than healthy ones, and barely have ten minutes left in your week to actually practice the magical work that is so important to you.

If any of this sounds like something you struggle with, you can try doing this spell for balance.

· · · SPELL 38 · · ·
Balance

You will need a pen and paper, a black candle and a white candle, and some symbol of time. This can be your watch, a clock, or a calendar. Or your phone, if you use that instead of one or more of the other things.

Take the paper and write down all the places in your life where you need balance. For instance, "Less work, more fun with friends," and so on. Put your list on your altar or table underneath your symbol for time and light

the black and white candles. Take a few minutes to visualize as strongly as you can making the changes on your list.
See yourself having fun, working out, eating healthier,
being more patient with your children, whichever items
you need more of in your life. Then say the spell. When
you are done, post the list where you will see it or leave
it on your altar if you have one and burn the candles a
little bit every day until they are gone to remind you of
your goal. You can repeat the spell each time if you want,
or not.

More of this and less of that
Less of that and more of this
Help me balance out my life
Give me back the things I miss
More light here and less dark there
Less dark there and more light here
Help me balance out my life
And down a middle path I'll steer
Balance! Balance! Balance!
So mote it be

Chapter Thirteen

SPELLCRAFTING AND CRAFTS

One of my favorite forms of spellcrafting involves combining a spell with a witchy craft so you have a solid reminder of your goals or a usable magical tool. I've done a few of these earlier in the book, but I thought I'd give you another set of spellcrafting crafts to play with before we finish. My coven is a very crafty bunch, so we often do some kind of craft to boost our magical work.

Putting a spell together with a witchy craft isn't just fun (although fun is good), but it also gives you an opportunity to really put your energy and intent into the item you're making. If you create your magical item slowly, concentrating on its purpose, that makes it even more powerful when you add in your spell.

In the earlier section on tools, I listed a number of items that many witches find helpful in boosting their focus and power while doing spellcraft. In this section, we'll explore some simple ones to make yourself. Try a few that appeal to you most, and see if you can feel the difference when you use something magical you created with intention.

• • • ACTIVITY 16 • • •
Book of Shadows

It can be said that a Book of Shadows is a witch's most precious possession, although not everyone uses one. They come in all different shapes and sizes and designs, but basically they are where a witch keeps magical knowledge. This can be anything from spells, to information on herbs and crystals, to divination results, dreams, even recipes for feast food or kitchen magic. Some are simple and linear (starting at the beginning of the book and just continuing through to the end). Others are organized into sections and added to here and there.

The kind of Book of Shadows you make will depend in part on how you intend to use it, but this is a basic approach. Remember that your Book is very personal and individual, and you want it to reflect your own magical practice. As with most other witchy things, there is no one right way, just what works for you.

Materials you'll need will include some or all of the following: a blank book or notebook with a plain cover, anything you want to use to decorate it with (dried flowers and leaves, pictures of anything witchy, feathers, magical symbols, ribbons, glitter, stone chips—anything that can be glued or tied onto the front), colored markers, decoupage glue or regular white glue thinned out with water. It might be easier to start with a book with a light-colored cover, unless you plan to cover it with a heavy paper or some kind of lightweight fabric in a neutral color, or use metallic markers that will show up on a darker background.

Gather all your materials and spend some time decorating the front of your Book of Shadows.

A Book of Shadows is an extension of the witch whose knowledge resides inside and should never be handled by someone else without permission.

You may want to lay everything out first to see how it looks before you fasten it down permanently by spreading glue on top of the flat bits and gluing anything larger on top of those. As you work, think about your magical path and how this Book will be part of it. Either on the outside cover or the inside front page, you will probably want to put "this Book belongs to" and either your mundane or your magical name, if you have one.

When you're done, you can bless and consecrate the Book if you choose.

• • • SPELL 39 • • •
Book of Shadows Blessing

This would be a good time to experiment with writing your own spell. A tool blessing is fairly simple, and there is no wrong approach. Here is the one I used for my own Book of Shadows (and which was printed in *The Eclectic Witch's Book of Shadows*). Maybe it will inspire you to try coming up with your own.

Bless this Book

In the name of the God and the Goddess

Who guide my feet on the Path of Beauty

Let it be filled with wisdom and knowledge

Let me use it only for good

Let me share it with those who need it

Let it help me grow in my Craft

And in my life

So mote it be

☽

Dreams can be used as a form of divination when they are approached with that purpose. Witches sometimes use dream sachets or charm bags to help them perform dream divination work. A dream sachet is basically a small fabric bag or pillow that is filled with herbs and other items and tucked underneath your regular pillow with the intention of bringing on meaningful dreams. The sachet can be used with or without the spell. Some people even like to write down the spell on a small piece of parchment or regular paper and tuck it into the sachet itself. (That's what I do.)

· · · ACTIVITY 17 · · ·

Dream Divination Sachet

You will need the following: a rectangular piece of cloth around three inches by four inches and a needle and thread (you can use a drawstring bag instead if you don't like to sew), various herbs (chamomile, lavender, catnip, and/or mugwort are the most commonly used, but you might want to leave out the catnip if you have cats that might be attracted to it, and mugwort can be a little intense to those who are sensitive, so it is fine to just use lavender if you prefer), a small amethyst crystal, paper and pen.

Fold the fabric over and sew up two sides so only one side is left open. Put in whatever herb or herbs you are using, along with the stone. You can write the spell that follows onto the paper, or the particular issue you are seeking answers to, if there is one. Or both. Either fold or roll up the paper and put it inside the sachet and close off the final side so you have a small pillow. If you want to get fancy, you can use the thread to "write" your initials or any other symbols on the outside.

When you are ready for bed, you can say the following spell over it or simply hold it in your hands for a few minutes and think about what you would like to learn from your dreams. Then tuck it under your pillow and sleep, perchance to dream.

Note: You can put a drop or two of lavender essential oil on the pillow to give it some extra oomph, especially if you are reusing it later.

• • • SPELL 40 • • •
Dream Divination

Say these words before sleep:

> Morpheus, let me sleep deep
> And dream true
> Apollo, send me knowledge
> That comes from you
> Dream pillow magic
> And sacred divination
> Bring to me answers
> And bright illumination

• • • ACTIVITY 18 • • •
Healing Candle

Candles are used in all sorts of magical work, but this is one application I particularly like and use fairly often. This example creates a candle for healing, but you can make one for any magical goal by changing up the herbs,

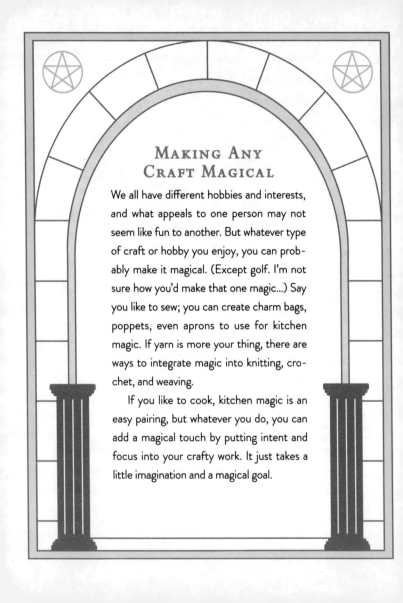

MAKING ANY CRAFT MAGICAL

We all have different hobbies and interests, and what appeals to one person may not seem like fun to another. But whatever type of craft or hobby you enjoy, you can probably make it magical. (Except golf. I'm not sure how you'd make that one magic...) Say you like to sew; you can create charm bags, poppets, even aprons to use for kitchen magic. If yarn is more your thing, there are ways to integrate magic into knitting, crochet, and weaving.

If you like to cook, kitchen magic is an easy pairing, but whatever you do, you can add a magical touch by putting intent and focus into your crafty work. It just takes a little imagination and a magical goal.

oils, and symbols you use, and then saying a slightly different spell.

You will need a pillar candle (you can use white or a color that matches your intention—healing might be blue, for example), various healing herbs (like calendula, lavender, lemon balm, chamomile, rose, thyme, rosemary, and peppermint—you can use only one, or a few, and you will probably want to crush them up so they are fairly small so they will spread more easily) and/or a magical healing oil, white glue, waxed paper, and a small pointed object like a toothpick or an athame for etching with.

There are a number of ways to do this, and you can include all the steps or leave out the ones that don't appeal to you. If you use a wide pillar candle, it should be safe to coat the outside with herbs since these types of candles rarely burn all the way to the outer edges. Otherwise you can use the oil instead or limit the herbs to the lower third of the candle to avoid the possibility of them catching on fire.

I like to start by etching healing symbols into the candle with a toothpick or some other pointed object. (Even your fingernail will work.) I use a few Norse runes (Uraz, Kenaz, Sigel, Tir, and Ing), maybe the outline of my body or the place that needs particular help if there is one, and my name or initials, a pentacle, and so on. You'll probably want to do this over the paper because it can be messy as the bits of wax drop off.

If you are using the dried herbs, spread a thin layer of glue on the outside of the candle. Spread the herbs out on the waxed paper and roll the candle gently through the herbs, patting them into place if necessary. Some people don't like the idea of using glue, in which case you can warm the sides of the candle until they are slightly soft and then roll it through the herbs. If you want to get fancy, you can make a pattern from the different herbs, but you can also just mix them all together. If you are actually making your own candle from scratch, you can even put some small pieces of healing crystals inside!

> Candles are one of the most versatile magical tools there is, and you can leave them out in plain sight.

Remember as you are doing this to focus on your goal of healing in whichever form you need it. If you are using essential oils instead of magical oils or healing herbs in dried form, you can anoint the candle with them, being careful to avoid the wick since they are flammable.

chapter thirteen

Once your candle has dried, you can use it with or without the following spell. If the issue is serious, you may want to burn it for a few moments every day, being careful to keep an eye on it because of the herbs.

· · · SPELL 41 · · ·
Healing II

This spell can be used with the previous healing candle or in any other healing magical work. Focus clearly on your intention for health and healing and say these words:

God and Goddess, hear my plea

Send me health and clarity

Help me heal and feel my best

Filled with energy and with zest

Take away hurt and disease

Sending me healing if you please

So mote it be

Chapter Fourteen
MEDITATIONS AND PRAYERS

Whenever I try to explain what a spell is to non-witchy folks, I tell them it is a lot like a prayer. After all, you are asking the gods (or the universe, or the powers that be) for help with something, most of the time. That's pretty much what a prayer is. Except with less sage and fewer crystals.

However, there are times when witches use what we consider to be actual prayers that are slightly different than spells. Usually these are simply spoken words with no magical actions to accompany them. Sometimes they're written out ahead of time, sometimes just spoken from the heart.

They may be addressed to a specific deity—especially if you have one you work with all the time or if there is one who is especially suitable for whatever the problem is—or just to Goddess, or Goddess and God. As always, there is no wrong way.

Unlike spells, prayers rarely rhyme, and while the full moon is always the perfect time to talk to the Goddess, there is no "right" time to say any particular prayer. You just say them when you need to. Also unlike spells, prayers are rarely repeated night after night. Once you have asked for whatever it is, you just have faith and hope and let it go.

That being said, any of the spells in this book can be treated like prayers and said on their own, if that's what works for you. Here are a few samples of witchy prayers, but I highly recommend trying to come up with a few of your own.

Prayer for Serenity

Goddess, grant me peace
As I walk through a world filled with chaos

Help me stay grounded

When the winds of change blow

Let me meet hate with love

And anger with calmness

And grant me serenity

As I walk through my days

Blessed be

Prayer for the World

God and Goddess, father and mother to us all

Please help our troubled world heal

Let fighting cease and diseases be cured

Mend the damage we have done to our planet

And show us how to live more gently on the earth

Help me be the best person I can be

A part of the solution and not the problem

God and Goddess, please heal the world

So mote it be

You can say this one every day if you want, all things considered.

Prayer for Healing

Great Goddess

Heal my body of all that ails it

Heal my heart of all that ails it

Heal my mind of all that ails it

Heal my spirit of all that ails it

Help me let go of all those things

That no longer work for my benefit

So I might heal in every aspect of my self

Great Goddess

Let me be healed

• • • ACTIVITY 19 • • •
Write Your Own Prayer

Think about some issue in your life you need help with and write a prayer to ask for deity's assistance. As you can see from the other prayers in this section, it doesn't have to be complicated or long. If you want, you don't even have to write it down. Just stand outside under the full moon or light a candle on your altar and speak from the heart.

Meditations are a way to dig deep, to put aside the cares of the world for a while and immerse yourself in the world of the spirit. My coven often uses meditations as a part of ritual, with one person leading and all the others sitting or standing with their eyes closed, listening and following along. They are a great tool for moving from the mundane world into the magical one, but they are also helpful during times of stress or when you just need to take a moment or two to catch your breath.

> The full moon is the perfect time to get together with other witches if you are inclined to work with others and lucky enough to have them around.

Like spells, they tap into a level of power and focus, but instead of aiming that focus outward, you turn it inward instead. If you find it difficult to get to the desired mental state if you are reading the meditation to yourself, silently or aloud, you can either record it and play it back or find meditations that are recorded by others.

There are meditations that are good for specific occasions like sabbats or the full moon, meditations that are intended to deal with specific issues like stress or fear or anxiety, and those that are good for helping you connect to the earth, the elements, or some other aspect of the magical world.

There are also guided meditations that lead you on a spiritual journey of some kind. In those cases, there is usually someone else speaking (either in person or on a recording) who leads you through the journey and back again.

Keep in mind that you can always change "you" to "me" if you are reading one for yourself. You can also skip the instructions to close your eyes and take a deep breath and just take the deep breath. (Obviously, it is hard to read the meditation if your eyes are closed! So you might want to record it and play it back for yourself.) If you are more comfortable just sitting back and listening to someone else reading a meditation and following along, you can find plenty of options online.

Here is an example of a basic meditation I often use during the summer solstice ritual.

Meditation on the Earth and Sun

Close your eyes. Take a deep, slow breath. Now another. Feel the strength of the earth underneath you. Solid and dependable, that strength is always there for you to call on if you need it. In your mind's eye, see yourself putting roots down into the ground, coming out of your tailbone or the soles of your feet, reaching deeper and deeper, down through the soil, deeper and deeper, toward the core of the earth itself. Feel your roots reaching down into the earth and connecting with that strength, that energy for growth. Feel that energy climbing up from the earth, up through those roots and into your own core, filling you with strength and calm and focus.

Now, reach upward and feel the power and the clarity that come from above. The vibrant energy from the sun, the clarity from the sky. Breathe it into the deepest core of your being. Feel the energy of the sun as it races through your veins and recharges your physical, mental, and spiritual batteries. Feel the light washing away all your stresses and cares, leaving only strength and clarity, calm and focus.

You are one with the earth. You are one with the sun. You are at peace.

Finish with a few deep, slow breaths.

☽

This is a meditation you can use on the spring equinox, or Beltane, or any other time during the spring.

Spring Equinox Meditation

Close your eyes. Take a slow deep breath. Feel the peace of sacred space surround you. Take another slow breath, and let go of the tensions of the everyday world. These things have no place here. Here there is only calm, and silence, and love.

> It is one thing to ask for help and another to be greedy, so try to keep your requests reasonable.

Listen to the slow breathing of those around you, if you are with others. Or listen to your own breathing. If you listen carefully, you can hear the breathing of the earth as she awakens. The birds call. The trees rustle. The earth stirs.

Send your awareness down. Down into the ground, into the dirt and the soil. Even if you are inside, the ground is still beneath you, under the floor, under your feet. Feel the roots of the trees shifting deep within the earth. Feel the small, subtle stirrings of the bulbs and the seeds. They have lain dormant all winter, storing their energy, waiting for their time to grow and blossom.

Now that time has come. All around us, the earth is coming back to life, rising, stretching, growing. Reach out for that energy. Feel it with all your senses—full of potential, unlimited, positive, and powerful. It is there, just waiting for you, patient like the earth, as limitless as nature herself.

Open your whole self to this beneficial energy. Let yourself be one with the potential for change and growth, health, prosperity, abundance, and joy. Feel the energy in your head, in your chest, in your belly, tingling in your fingers and toes.

Send gratitude out to our mother the earth for this gift, and fill yourself to overflowing with the bountiful energy of spring. Feel yourself begin to blossom and grow, and know that all things are possible.

This is a meditation that works well for the night of the full moon or anytime you feel the desire to connect with the Goddess, the moon, and your own witchy energy. It should be done at night, and outside if possible. If you can't see the moon or the stars, use your imagination. They're still up there, even if you're inside or the sky is cloudy.

Moon Meditation for Magical Connection

It is night, the time for magic. The moon sails through the dark sky, and stars dance above, twinkling with light that has traveled millions of years to get here. Take a deep breath and feel the magic in the air. Energy flows down from above, filled with the potential for wonder and witchcraft, just waiting for you to reach out and grasp it. Breathe it in. Breathe it out.

The Goddess waits too, her arms open and her heart filled with unconditional love for all witches, for we are her children. Reach out to her with your spirit and feel her gentle touch upon your face, like moonbeams reaching down to caress you with the power of a thousand suns. Breathe it in. Breathe it out.

Feel the legacy of generations of witches who went before you, who walked their paths of magic and felt the same pull of the moon, the same call of the Goddess, the same gifts of nature. Feel them reach down through the centuries to lend you their power so you might walk in their footsteps and create a path of your own for others to follow in their own time. Breathe it in. Breathe it out.

Feel the energy of the moon, of the Goddess, of the magic that flows through your veins, and know that you are a witch, a child of the wild woods and the night sky. Feel yourself fill with power. Breathe it in. Breathe it out. Be the magic.

Conclusion

Being a witch means something different to everyone, but at its core, it is how you see your place in the universe, how you choose and walk your path through life, what you believe, and how you use those beliefs to deal with good times and bad.

For most witches, it also colors how we connect to nature, to others, to ourselves, and, in the end, to that invisible power that is magic. Witchcraft gives us the opportunity to shape the world around us and create positive change in our lives, and hopefully in the lives of those we care for. It allows us to follow a spiritual path that fits our own personal needs and personalities, which the religions we grew up with may not have.

There is much more to Witchcraft than spells, but for many of us, they are an important and powerful component of our magical practice. They give us a way to connect with the gods, to delve deep into our own power, and to strengthen our magical muscles.

Spellcraft helps us channel our goals and desires into concrete actions designed to bring about specific results. There are no guarantees we will get what we want— sometimes we don't quite get it right, or we're asking for the wrong thing, or the answer is just plain no, but with focus, intent, and belief, we work our magic in the hope of creating the desired outcome, and more times than not, it actually happens.

While you can always use a spell written by someone else, with or without incorporating your own personal touches, there is a certain power in creating your own spells, crafted with your own words out of your own passion. Every bit of yourself that you put into crafting a spell—from choosing the tools and ingredients you will use to coming up with the words that reflect what lies in your own heart—adds to the potent magic generated when you perform it.

Even if you don't feel confident in your ability to write spells, everyone can do it. I promise. Sometimes it just takes practice and faith and embracing your own power as a witch. This, after all, is at the core of a Witchcraft life lived well. Keep working at your Craft, try different approaches to see what works for you, and before you know it, spellcrafting will be an integral part of your magical toolbox.

I hope you have found this book fun and helpful and at least a little bit inspiring, and that you will go on to craft your own spells, channeling your inner witch into words of magic. Use a wand, or not. It's up to you. Because really all you need is heart and spirit and faith, and I already know you have that in abundance.

Happy spellcrafting.

Deborah
Blake

CORRESPONDENCES

There are entire books filled with correspondences, but this is a basic list that will help you get started with some of the most common forms of spellcasting.

Prosperity and Abundance

GODS AND GODDESSES: Ceres, Demeter, Fortuna, Freya, Saturn, the Dagha

STONES: Aventurine, bloodstone, citrine, jade, malachite, tiger's eye, turquoise

HERBS: Basil, cinnamon, clove, dill, ginger, patchouli, peppermint, sandalwood

COLOR: Green

RUNE SYMBOLS: Fehu, Daeg, Othel, Gifu, Uraz, Tir

Protection

GODS AND GODDESSES: Bastet, Bes, Hemdall, Isis, Sekhmet, Thor

STONES: Agate, amber, amethyst, black onyx, carnelian, citrine, crystal quartz, garnet, jade, jet, lapis, malachite, moonstone, red jasper, turquoise

HERBS: Basil, chamomile, cinnamon, dill, eucalyptus, garlic, geranium, juniper, parsley, rose, rosemary, sage

COLORS: Black, white

RUNE SYMBOLS: Thurisaz, Eihwaz, Eolh, Kenaz

Healing and Peace

GODS AND GODDESSES: Apollo, Belenus, Brigit, Eir, Isis, Kuan Yin, Morpheus, Nuada, Rhiannon

STONES: Amber, amethyst, aventurine, bloodstone, carnelian, crystal quartz, fluorite, garnet, hematite, jade, jasper, jet, lapis, malachite, onyx, smoky quartz, sodalite, turquoise

HERBS: Apple, calendula, catnip, chamomile, dill, eucalyptus, geranium, lavender, lemon balm, peppermint, rose, rosemary, thyme

COLORS: Blue, black (to banish illness), green (growth)

RUNE SYMBOLS: Uraz, Kenas, Sigel, Tir, Ing

Love

GODS AND GODDESSES: Aengus, Aphrodite, Astarte, Bastet, Cupid, Eros, Freya, Hathor, Inanna, Ishtar, Isis

STONES: Agate, amethyst, garnet, jade, lapis, malachite, moonstone, rose quartz, turquoise

HERBS: Apple, basil, calendula, carnation, catnip, chamomile, cinnamon, clove, geranium, lavender, lemon, lemon balm, rose, thyme

When casting a love spell, be very, very careful not to do anything that would interfere with the free will of anyone else.

COLORS: Pink (romantic love), red (passionate love)

RUNE SYMBOLS: Fehu, Kenaz, Gifu, Wunjo, Beorc, Ing

Strength and Courage

GODS AND GODDESSES: Ares, Artemis, Diana, Inanna, Isis, Tyr

STONES: Agate (especially orange and red), amethyst, carnelian, citrine, lapis, tiger's eye

HERBS: Allspice, apple, basil, cinnamon, clove, frankincense, lemon, patchouli, pine, sage, thyme

COLORS: Bright yellow, orange, red

RUNE SYMBOLS: Uruz, Kenaz, Sigel

Intuition and Psychic Power

GODS AND GODDESSES: Apollo, Brigid, Cerridwin, Frigg, Janus, Hecate

STONES: Amber, amethyst, blue lace agate, crystal quartz, lapis, moonstone

HERBS: Chamomile, frankincense, ginger, lavender, myrrh, patchouli, rosemary, sage, vervain

COLORS: Purple, silver

RUNE SYMBOLS: Ansuz, Lagaz, Mannaz, Perdhro

GLOSSARY

These are some common terms used in Witchcraft you may not be familiar with.

BANISHING: Banishing means to get rid of something. Things we may wish to banish include physical, psychological, and spiritual issues, or even people. Be very careful if you use magic to banish someone from your life, as it is rarely an action that can be taken back. Banishing is useful as an adjunct to practical work to improve our lives.

BLESSING: We bless tools, spaces, and even ourselves. Generally, we are asking the gods or the universe to send their blessings on our endeavors, spells, or belongings. It adds an element of power and the sacred to whatever it is you are blessing.

> Find the aspects of any holiday that appeal to you the most and celebrate them with spells or ritual.

CAKES AND ALE: This is both the part of the ritual where some form of food and drink are used to ground you back to the mundane world or make an offering to the gods (usually coming right before the end) and the name for the food and drink itself. "Ale" isn't necessarily something alcoholic, and cake doesn't have to be cake. It is just the general term for whatever we choose to use. Often this may be bread, or a cookie, and wine or juice.

CLEANSING AND CLEARING: In magical work, we often begin by clearing the energy of people or places or things. You might cleanse your sacred space or circle before you say a spell or clear a new tool, especially if it belonged to someone previously and you want to rid it of any leftover energy to make room for your own.

CONSECRATE: Consecrating is related to blessing, but it is more that you are pledging whatever is being consecrated (a new tool, a charm bag, a tarot deck) to positive magical use.

DEDICATION: Dedication is usually the act of making a formal commitment in spiritual form. While it is more associated with covens, some witches choose to self-dedicate to the Craft when they feel they are ready to formally commit themselves to following that path.

DEITY: A general word for any god or goddess.

DEOSIL: Movement done in a clockwise direction sometimes for increase or positive work or to close a circle.

Divination: Divination involves searching for answers or for knowledge of the future. Tools used for divination include tarot cards, rune stones, oracle cards, scrying, pendulums, and more.

Element: Earth, air, fire, and water are the four elements that are used in spellwork and other magical endeavors. They are also referred to as elemental powers, and some witches see them as actual beings or energies. Spirit is sometimes considered a fifth element and is represented by the fifth point on the pentacle.

Esbat: Esbat is the name for the lunar rituals, usually associated with the full moon.

Intent: This term refers to both the purpose of a spell or magical working as well as the focused energy used to bring it about. Intent is one of the main components of spellcasting.

Invocation: An invocation is a call, a prayer, or a summoning. When we talk about invocations in Witchcraft, it is usually associated with inviting the elements and/or the God/dess to come into our magical space.

LAW OF RETURNS: This is a generally accepted Wiccan precept that everything you put out into the universe comes back to you. So if you do positive magic, you will get positive things in return, but negative magic may come back to you in ways that will harm you.

PENTACLE: A commonly used Witchcraft symbol that consists of a five-pointed star with a circle around it. The five points represent the five elements: earth, air, fire, water, and spirit, and the circle is the universe that holds them all, or unity. A pentagram, which is closely related to the pentacle, is a five-pointed star (drawn in one continuous line). A pentacle is usually a physical item (such as a piece of jewelry) and a pentagram is usually drawn, but the terms can be used interchangeably.

QUARTER: These are directions used in magical work, and there are four, each with their own set of associations: east (air), south (fire), west (water), and north (earth).

QUARTER CALLS: The invocations we say to invite the powers of the quarters to enter our sacred space are referred to as quarter calls. They can vary from the extremely simple "Power of Air, please join me in my magical circle" to more elaborate invocations that call on special associations.

SABBAT: One of eight holidays in the Pagan calendar that includes the two solstices, two equinoxes, and four quarter-cross holidays that fall at equal times between them. They are Imbolc (Feb 2), Ostara (spring equinox, around March 21), Beltane (May 1), Midsummer (summer solstice, around June 21), Lammas (August 2), Mabon (autumn equinox, around September 21), Samhain (October 31), and Yule (winter solstice, around December 21).

> Yule and Christmas, as well as Chanukah, all celebrate the light, something we can come together over.

The dates of the solstices and equinoxes vary slightly every year.

SOLITARY: A witch who practices alone. Most witches who belong to a coven also do solitary work, but a solitary witch is one who always or almost always practices on their own, either out of choice or because they can't find anyone to share their magical work with.

WHEEL OF THE YEAR: The Pagan calendar of holidays and the turning of the seasons. Magical work is often done according to where on the Wheel of the Year we are, since the energy of the earth changes with the seasons.

WICCA: A modern form of Witchcraft practice brought over from England. It has since developed into many different variations, none of which follow exactly the same beliefs or tenets. All Wiccans are witches, but not all witches are Wiccans.

WIDDERSHINS: Movement that is done in a counterclockwise direction, usually used for banishing, unbinding, or for opening a magical circle at the end of a ritual.

TO WRITE TO THE AUTHOR

If you wish to contact the author or would like more information about this book, please write to the author in care of Llewellyn Worldwide and we will forward your request. Both the author and the publisher appreciate hearing from you and learning of your enjoyment of this book and how it has helped you. Llewellyn Worldwide cannot guarantee that every letter written to the author can be answered, but all will be forwarded.

Please write to:

Deborah Blake
℅ Llewellyn Worldwide
2143 Wooddale Drive
Woodbury, MN 55125-2989

Please enclose a self-addressed stamped envelope for reply or $1.00 to cover costs. If outside the USA, enclose an international postal reply coupon.